·FOOLPROOF·

SLOW COOKER

•FOOLPROOF•

SLOW COOKER

60 ESSENTIAL RECIPES THAT MAKE THE
MOST OF YOUR SLOW COOKER
REBECCA WOODS

PHOTOGRAPHY BY
RITA PLATTS

Hardie Grant

QUADRILLE

Publishing Director
Sarah Lavelle

Commissioning Editor
Stacey Cleworth

Series Designer
Emily Lapworth

Designer
Alicia House

Photographer
Rita Platts

Food Stylist
Rebecca Woods

Prop Stylist
Max Robinson

Head of Production
Stephen Lang

Senior Production Controller
Nikolaus Ginelli

First published in 2022 by Quadrille,
an imprint of Hardie Grant Publishing

Quadrille
52–54 Southwark Street
London SE1 1UN
quadrille.com

Text © Quadrille 2022
Photography © Rita Platts 2022
Design and layout © Quadrille 2022

Thanks to Lakeland for the brilliant slow cookers,
as photographed on pages 35 and 52.

Cataloguing in Publication Data: a catalogue
record for this book is available from the
British Library.

9781787138995

Printed in China

CONTENTS

INTRODUCTION

Slow cookers have long since been regarded as a great way to create economical meals, able as they are to render inexpensive cuts of meat – or cheap dried beans and pulses, for that matter – into tender deliciousness. But never before has the cost of cooking the meal itself been so relevant. As fuel prices soar, the slow cooker sits smugly on work surfaces, cooking delicious meals for just a few pence worth of energy. The slow cooker is very much having a renaissance.

But, rather unfairly, they haven't always been so in favour. Slow cooking very much went out of fashion for a couple of decades. The technique was associated with food that was mushy, brown and flavourless. And to be fair, some of it still is on the brown, homogenous side – sometimes, a bowl of hearty brown stew is exactly what's called for! Still, there's far more to slow cooking than that.

Our approach to food has moved on since slow cookers were in their heyday. While I was growing up in the 1980s, simple stews and soups (perfect slow cooker fare) were very much a staple, alongside meat and two veg and the odd weekend curry for a treat. Thankfully our food horizons have broadened immensely in the subsequent two decades and so slow cooking today is about catching up to changing tastes and finding ways to recreate these new favourites in a classic appliance.

Saying that, the cookers themselves have now become more sophisticated and lend themselves to cooking with a little more nuance than just shoving it all in and hoping for the best. You can set timers, which make them start cooking when you want them to, or reduce the heat and keep food warm when the cooking is finished. Modern metal bowl inserts make 'baking' cakes in slow cookers easier and some also allow you to place those bowls on the hob first so you can brown your meat in the same dish and save on washing up: the landscape is changing.

When I was researching for this book, I came across a long list of things you're not supposed to cook in a slow cooker – pasta, rice, fish and seafood, green vegetables, any dairy… I don't necessarily agree with this. You can make lovely rice and pasta dishes, you just have to approach them in a slightly different way and get used to your own slow cooker timings. If you add certain ingredients towards the end of cooking they are fine, and attempting less obvious dishes will massively broaden your dinner repertoire, rather than just using the device as a soup and casserole maker. But I do understand the appeal of filling a cooker and then being able to forget about it for hours, so there are a good number of those 'traditional' recipes here, too.

I hope you enjoy the recipes and give them a try, but first, a few tips to get you started…

Getting to know your slow cooker

Slow cookers come in a huge range of models – they can have a large or small capacity, be round or oval, digital or manual, have a ceramic bowl or a metal one.

I'm not going to go into huge detail about the process of choosing a slow cooker – the likelihood is, if you have this book in your hands, you are already the owner of one. But some of these characteristics do need to be kept in mind as you cook, so here is how to approach some of the recipes to adapt them to your slow cooker.

The main thing is to get to know your cooker. Without set temperatures, they all cook slightly differently. Love it and become familiar with its quirks, and it will reward you with bowls full of hearty meals.

Size and shape

Slow cookers come in an enormous array of sizes, from the small 1.5 litre (1½ quart) models suitable for one to two people, to large 6-litre (6¼-quart) ones that can cook a wholesome meal for a family of six and still leave you with leftovers. I have tested most of the recipes in this book in 3.5 litre (3½ quart) slow cookers, as they are the most common, and a meal from one of these will happily feed a family of four.

Even if you are just cooking for one, using the slow cooker is a brilliant way to batch cook, and most of the recipes in this book will freeze well – look for the freezer symbol '❄' on the page. If you do have a smaller cooker, you may find that simply halving a stew, soup, curry or casserole recipe will work.

There are also a few recipes that will require a large cooker. Large joints of meat such as whole lamb legs (see the Lamb Kleftiko recipe on page 34) or brisket (see the Smoky Korean BBQ Brisket recipe on page 24) will need more space, and an oval-shaped cooker is particularly useful for these as it's longer.

Additionally, if you want to use your cooker as a bain marie, to gently cook dishes such as Smoked Salmon and Spinach Egg Pots (see page 81), Raspberry, Vanilla and Dark Chocolate Cheesecake (see page 136), Individual Crème Brûlées (see page 138) or the

Haslet (see page 18), you will need a cooker big enough to fit another vessel (or multiple small dishes) inside. Having a slightly larger one will allow you to be more adventurous in your slow cooking.

Material

Your slow cooker will have either a ceramic bowl or a metal bowl insert. Please be aware that the metal ones will get hotter and will heat up much more quickly than ceramic ones. The time brackets provided with the recipes have been calculated to take this into account, but if you are cooking in a ceramic bowl and the dish isn't done by the end of the cooking time, do give it a bit longer. Likewise, if you have a cooker with a metal insert and it seems to be cooking more quickly, adjust the recipe next time to match your cooker.

On the subject of materials, cookers with glass lids are very handy as they enable you to see what's going on without having to lift the lid. Slow cookers do things rather silently, so sometimes it's nice to be able to see what's happening. You don't want to be lifting the lid too often – I explain why on page 9!

Digital or manual

Digital cookers that you can programme are useful if you want to cook a recipe for an extended time while you are away from home. Once the time is up, they will switch to a 'keep warm' setting that won't cook the food much more, but will keep it warm so you can eat it straight away when you are ready, and also keep the food at a safe temperature and prevent it from becoming a food poisoning risk. For soups, stews and large joints of meat, this is invaluable. But I would advise you not to keep dishes with more sensitive ingredients on this setting – rice and pasta will get very mushy, and fish is easy to overcook, so these should be removed from the cooker as soon as the cooking time is up.

Getting used to slow cooking

Using a slow cooker is simple, once you are aware of a few key rules. Begin with the recipes in the book and I'll guide you through, but once you start creating your own dishes, it will help to remember the following.

Preheat your cooker

It's good to get used to doing this. Even though modern slow cookers with metal inserts will heat up very quickly, getting your appliance to cooking temperature before adding your ingredients does help cut down on the margin of error, so I have specified to preheat all slow cookers in my recipes. It's not so important with soups, stews and other recipes with a long cooking time, but for some shorter recipes, preheating will make a difference to the final result, so do try and follow the guidance with the recipes. If I have stated a particular setting to heat it to, do also follow that.

Know your ingredients

If you want to use your slow cooker to prepare a wider range of dishes, it's worth knowing some of the issues with slow cooking certain foods. If they are cooked carefully, however, they can be enjoyed rather than avoided.

• **Meat** is at the centre of traditional slow cooker meals – and for good reason. Long slow cooking tenderizes meat and can turn cheaper, tougher cuts into meltingly tender bites. Avoid using traditional 'steak' cuts, such as sirloin or fillet, as these tend to require very hot, quick cooking to, ideally, be served still pink – something that your slow cooker will not deliver on. Likewise with chicken, cheaper thighs will generally give you better results than more expensive chicken breast fillets.

• **Fish** is very easy to overcook and become dry, but it can still be prepared succesfully in the slow cooker. Add it towards the end of the cooking time, for example in the Sweet and Sour King Prawns recipe (see page 77) or Creamy Seafood Chowder (see page 72) or just give it a shorter cooking time.

• **Some vegetables**, especially green ones such as peas, will come out of the slow cooker mushy, brown and unappealing if left for too long. As with fish, add these towards the end of the cooking time if you want them to retain a bit more colour and crunch.

• **Dairy** products can split if left in the cooker too long. To help prevent this, always use full fat dairy products, which are more stable, and add them towards the end of the cooking time.

• **Rice and pasta** can be cooked in the slow cooker, but not left for several hours, with the exception perhaps of the rice pudding. If you are happy to use your slow cooker more like a hob than something you walk away from, try the Jerk Turkey Rice (see page 63) or the Creamy Tuna and Pea Conchiglioni (see page 67) recipes.

Pre-preparing your food

Many dishes prepared in the slow cooker, especially meat, will benefit from a little pre-prep on the stovetop first. While some recipes will allow for chucking everything in and walking away, this may be how slow cooking got its reputation for being a little bland. A few careful minutes spent browning your meat, taking the overwhelming tang off garlic, or softening your onions will really pay off in the flavour and texture of your dish.

If you want to put your slow cooker on in the morning to cook throughout the day, you can always do the pre-prep (chopping veg, browning meat etc.) the night before and refrigerate your ingredients, ready to tip them into the cooker and turn it on just before you leave for the day.

Bump up the flavours

When you are slow cooking, flavours can often be a lot more muted than when cooking with higher heats. Therefore, you will notice on some recipes that the amount of spices that are called for might seem excessive, but they won't taste that strong once the dish is cooked. This goes for seasoning, too – taste each dish at the end of the cooking time and don't be afraid to add more salt and pepper if required.

Use less liquid

When you cook in a saucepan, you will lose a lot of the moisture in the form of steam; even with a lid on, it tends to escape. This doesn't happen when slow cooking as the lid makes a seal and the moisture is trapped inside the cooker. Therefore, most of the recipes in this book don't use a lot of extra liquid (unless, of course, they are intended to be watery, like soups or stews). Many people believe that meat and vegetables need to be submerged in water when they are slow cooked, but that's not the case; the whole environment in a slow cooker is damp, so they will be fine with just a little liquid, and the flavours will be more concentrated.

Thickening stews etc.

As liquid doesn't evaporate in a slow cooker, you will need to thicken stews using other methods. Start with less liquid (see above) and try adding cornflour (cornstarch) to your recipe; combine it with a little liquid to form a paste before adding (otherwise you'll end up with a lumpy mess). This will thicken the dish as it cooks. If it is not thickened to your liking by the end of the cooking time, you can scoop out a couple of ladlefuls of the liquid and put it in a saucepan on the hob. Mix a little cornflour with a splash of cold water and add it to the pan, then cook for a couple of minutes

on the hob until it starts to thicken, but don't cook for too long – it needs to be a loose consistency or it won't combine with the liquid in your cooker. Stir the thickened liquid back into the slow cooker and cook for a few minutes longer. Rice, potatoes and other starchy foods will also help to thicken liquids, for example the Chicken Mulligatawny (see page 53), is thickened with rice, and potatoes help to add body to the Creamy Seafood Chowder (see page 72).

Don't peek too much

Every time you remove the slow cooker lid, you set the cooking time back a good 10–15 minutes. This isn't a huge problem with soups, stews, large joints of meat and other less sensitive dishes – apart from having to wait a bit longer for your dinner – but if you're trying a recipe for a cake, it might make a difference to the final result. Invest in a slow cooker with a glass lid, so you can satisfy yourself that things are happening by peeking through the glass rather than lifting the lid and letting all the heat escape.

Storing slow cooked food

Don't leave food sitting in the bowl of the slow cooker once cooked. Pasta, rice and any of the 'baking' dishes will continue to cook in the residual heat and become overcooked. For other dishes, it may mean they cool too slowly to be safely stored as the bowl will retain heat for a long time. Instead, serve up your food and decant any leftovers into a cold container to cool quickly, then refrigerate.

As I've mentioned, most of the recipes in this book will freeze well. Slow cooking is a brilliant way to cook large batches of healthy, homemade 'ready meals'. Decant the cooked food into portion-sized containers and pop them in the freezer.

Now, on to the recipes!

MEAT

Cooking meat is really where slow cookers come into their own, rendering joints meltingly tender with such ease, leaving you more time to think about the flavours you can add – and there is inspiration from around the world here. Try a Moroccan-inspired lamb shank tagine, classic Italian meatballs, a spicy brisket smothered in Korean gochujang, or a humble meatloaf from Lincolnshire in the UK!

POLISH SMOKED SAUSAGE HOTPOT *

Deeply smoky sausages, rich dried mushrooms and sweet onions and cabbage make this rustic stew richly filling. Serve simply with buttered crusty bread to mop up the juices.

20g (⅔oz) dried mushrooms,
    such as chanterelle or porcini
2 large onions, sliced
150g (5½oz) spicy kabanos sausage,
    sliced into 2.5cm (1in) lengths
500g (1lb 2oz) smoked podwawelska
    sausage, sliced into thick discs
300g (10½oz) button chestnut
    (cremini) mushrooms, halved
    or quartered if large
650ml (22fl oz/2¾ cups) Polish lager
1½ tsp caraway seeds
1 tsp crushed juniper berries
2 chicken stock pots
½ small white cabbage, sliced
sea salt and freshly ground black
    pepper
crusty bread, to serve

Preheat the slow cooker.

Put the dried mushrooms in a jug and pour over 200ml (7fl oz/scant 1 cup) boiling water. Let them soak while you prep the rest of the hotpot.

Add all the remaining ingredients to the slow cooker, then strain in the mushroom soaking liquid through a sieve to catch any gritty bits. Put the soaked mushrooms onto a chopping board and chop roughly, then add these to the slow cooker. If you have a 3-litre (3-quart) cooker, it will be quite a squeeze, but as long as you can get the lid on, it's fine. The ingredients will all wilt down as they cook.

Cook the stew for 7 hours on LOW, or 3½ hours on HIGH – the cabbage should be well wilted and tender. Taste and season with salt and pepper. Serve with crusty bread.

Serves 6
–
Prep 30 mins
–
Cook 3½–7 hours

PORK PAPRIKASH ✻

A twist on a classic Hungarian dish, the paprika – delicious although not entirely traditional – lends this stew a sweet smoky flavour. Serve with pasta, noodles or gnocchi.

1–2 tbsp olive oil
500g (1lb 2oz) pork steaks, sliced into
    1.5cm (½in) thick strips
1 onion, finely sliced
2 garlic cloves, finely chopped
1 chicken stock pot
2 red peppers, deseeded and sliced
1 × 400g (14oz) can chopped tomatoes
2 tbsp smoked sweet paprika
150g (5½oz) full fat crème fraîche or
    soured cream
sea salt and freshly ground black
    pepper

To serve
pappardelle pasta or gnocchi
chopped parsley

Preheat the slow cooker.

Heat 1 tablespoon of the oil in a large non-stick frying pan over a very high heat and quickly brown half the pork until golden and caramelized on the outside. Transfer to the slow cooker with tongs and repeat to cook the remaining pork, adding the second tablespoon of oil if needed.

Add the onion to the pan and cook for a few minutes until starting to soften and colour, then add the garlic and give it another minute before adding to the slow cooker.

Add the stock pot, peppers, tomatoes and paprika to the slow cooker and season well with salt and pepper. Pop the lid on and cook for 3 hours on HIGH or 6 hours on LOW.

Stir in the crème fraîche or soured cream and taste to check the seasoning. Serve with pappardelle pasta or gnocchi, sprinkled with the parsley.

Serves 4
–
Prep 20 mins
–
Cook 3–6 hours

Meat

15

SAUSAGE, BEAN & FENNEL CASSEROLE ✳

If you can find proper meaty Italian fennel sausages for this, it will be well worth the hunt for that hit of aniseedy flavour. Try an Italian deli for these, if you can stretch to it. If not, it's a pretty tasty stew regardless.

250g (9oz) dried cannellini beans, soaked in water overnight, then drained
2 tbsp olive oil
12 Italian fennel sausages
2 tsp fennel seeds
1 onion, finely sliced
2 large garlic cloves, finely sliced
1 very large or 2 smaller fennel bulbs, sliced into wedges, or 6 baby fennel bulbs, halved
2 carrots, peeled and diced
2 celery sticks, diced
200ml (7fl oz/scant 1 cup) white wine
1 sprig of rosemary
1 chicken stock pot
700g (1lb 9oz) passata
fresh parsley leaves, to serve (optional)
sea salt and freshly ground black pepper

The night before you want to make the casserole, pop the dried beans in a bowl and cover well with water. Leave to soak overnight.

The next day, preheat the slow cooker.

Add 1 tablespoon of the oil to a frying pan set over a high heat and brown the sausages all over. Using tongs, transfer them to the slow cooker, leaving the oil in the pan.

Reduce the heat to medium, add the fennel seeds and onion to the pan and cook for a few minutes until they are picking up some colour and the onion is softened. Add the garlic and cook for another minute or so, then tip into the slow cooker.

Add the remaining oil to the pan and fry the fennel wedges for a few minutes, turning occasionally, until lightly browned. Tip them into the slow cooker and add the beans, carrots, celery, white wine, rosemary and chicken stock pot. Add the passata, then fill the bottle one-third full with water, swill it around to pick up all the remaining tomato juice, and add that too. Season with a good pinch of salt and pepper.

Cook the casserole on LOW for 6–7 hours or HIGH for 3–4 hours, or until the beans are tender. Taste and adjust the seasoning, then serve, sprinkled with parsley, if you like.

Tip
Some dried beans take longer to soften than others, depending on how long they have been stored for. If the cannellini beans are not tender at the end of the cooking time, keep cooking until they soften – this dish benefits from a long cook.

Serves 6
–
Prep 25 mins
–
Cook 3–7 hours

HASLET (AKA SANDWICH MEATLOAF) *

Meatloaf is a great dish to cook in the slow cooker as it doesn't dry out. This is a British-style loaf – rather than the more typical American ones – called 'haslet' locally in Lincolnshire, where I spent time with my grandparents as a child. Rather than serving it hot with veg, haslet is usually served cold, sliced and in sandwiches or with a salad. Traditionally it was made in a Christmas pudding shape and wrapped in caul to hold it together, but I have made it into a loaf as it's easier to slice, and wrapped it in smoked bacon as it's more available and imparts a lovely smoky flavour.

20g (⅔oz) butter
1 large red onion, finely diced
16 slices streaky bacon (about 240g/8½oz)
700g (1lb 9oz) minced (ground) pork belly
150g (5½oz) minced (ground) pork liver
1½ tbsp dried sage
2 tsp dried thyme
½ tsp ground nutmeg
1 tsp fine salt
1 tsp freshly ground black pepper
1 egg, beaten
60g (2oz) dried breadcrumbs (I use panko crumbs)

Preheat the slow cooker to LOW.

Melt the butter in a frying pan over low–medium heat and add the onion. Cook for a good 8 minutes until it is really soft but not coloured, then turn off the heat and allow to cool.

Meanwhile, line a 900g (2lb) loaf pan with cling film (plastic wrap), leaving plenty overhanging at the sides. Use 12 of the bacon slices to line the tin, so the base and sides are completely covered.

Put the pork belly and liver in a large bowl and add the cooled onions, sage, thyme, nutmeg, salt, pepper, egg and breadcrumbs. Mix everything together well, then pack the mixture into the lined pan. Fold any overhanging bacon over the top of the loaf and use the remaining bacon slices to cover the top, then fold over the overhanging cling film to seal. Cover the top of the tin with a sheet of foil.

Put the loaf tin into the slow cooker and pour in enough hot water from the kettle to come two-thirds of the way up the sides. Replace the lid and cook for about 6 hours, until the loaf is firm and cooked through. Allow to cool in the tin.

Remove the haslet from the tin and slice to serve in sandwiches (delicious with apple sauce!) or with salad.

Tip

The easiest way to source your meat for this is to talk nicely to your butcher; if I give my lovely local guys a bit of notice, they will put the pork belly and liver through the mincer together for me. If not, you can buy them separately and just finely chop or blend the pork belly and liver together at home. Or just sub the liver for more pork belly mince – although the liver really does add to the traditional flavour.

Makes 1 large loaf
–
Prep 30 mins
–
Cook 6 hours

CLASSIC ITALIAN MEATBALLS ❄

Meatballs are so tender when cooked in a slow cooker, and they will happily cook along with their sauce, cutting down on work – bonus.

2 tbsp olive oil
1 onion, finely diced
3 garlic cloves, finely chopped
400g (14oz) passata
1 × 400g (14oz) can chopped tomatoes
a small handful of fresh basil leaves,
    torn, plus extra to serve
cooked spaghetti, to serve

For the meatballs
250g (9oz) minced (ground) pork
250g (9oz) minced (ground) beef
½ tbsp dried basil
1 tsp dried flat-leaf parsley
2 garlic cloves, crushed
½ tsp red chilli flakes
30g (1oz) dried breadcrumbs
30g (1oz) Parmesan cheese, finely
    grated, plus extra to serve
sea salt and freshly ground black
    pepper

Preheat the slow cooker.

To make the meatballs, combine all the ingredients in a large mixing bowl and season with a good amount of salt and pepper. Mix everything together with a spoon, then get your hands in there and mash it together to make sure the mixture is well combined. Divide it into 16 equal portions and roll each into a ball.

Heat the oil in a large non-stick frying pan over medium–high heat and add the meatballs. Fry for a few minutes, turning regularly with tongs, until browned all over, then transfer to the slow cooker, leaving the oil in the pan. You may need to brown them in two batches, depending on the size of your pan.

Turn the heat under the frying pan down to low–medium and add the onion and garlic to the pan. Sauté gently for a few minutes until beginning to soften and turn translucent, then tip everything into the slow cooker. Add the passata, then quarter fill its container with water, swill the water around to pick up all the remaining tomato juice, and tip it into the slow cooker. Repeat with the chopped tomatoes.

Season with salt and pepper and pop a lid on the slow cooker. Cook for 3–4 hours on HIGH or 6–7 hours on LOW. Taste and check the seasoning, then stir in the basil and serve the meatballs and sauce on top of spaghetti, or a pasta of your choice, sprinkled with Parmesan and more fresh basil leaves.

Serves 4
–
Prep 40 mins
–
Cook 3–7 hours

Meat

HEARTY OXTAIL SOUP ✳

This really is a slow, two-step process, but it's worth it for the most comforting, satisfying soup – almost a stew, in fact – you'll ever try. I have purposely scaled up the recipe to make eight portions as this takes a little more effort, but you can freeze any leftovers. You will need a large 6-litre (6¼-quart) slow cooker to fit it all in. If not, just halve the recipe. Make it the day before and chill overnight. It will allow the flavours to develop, and will also mean you will be able to easily extract the fat from the top.

2 tbsp olive oil
1.5kg (3lb 5oz) oxtail
1 large onion, finely diced
1 tbsp soft brown sugar
3 garlic cloves, finely chopped
1½ tbsp chopped fresh rosemary
2 rich beef stock pots
2 carrots, finely diced
2 sticks celery, finely diced
1 × 400g (14oz) can chopped tomatoes
2 tbsp tomato purée (paste)
2 bay leaves
3 tbsp sweet sherry, marsala or
    madeira
1 handful of fresh thyme sprigs
1 tbsp Worcestershire sauce
sea salt and freshly ground black
    pepper
bread, to serve

Preheat the slow cooker to LOW.

Heat the oil in a large non-stick frying pan over a high heat and brown the oxtail joints all over. Transfer the meat to the slow cooker with tongs, leaving any fat in the pan.

Turn the heat under the frying pan right down to low and add the onion to the pan along with the brown sugar and a good pinch of salt. Sauté gently for 8–10 minutes until starting to caramelize, then add the garlic and rosemary. Cook for 2 more minutes, then tip into the slow cooker.

Dissolve the stock pots in 2 litres (2 quarts) of boiling water and pour into the slow cooker.

Add all the remaining ingredients along with a good pinch of salt and pepper and stir together, then cook on LOW for 8 hours. Leave to cool, then chill in the fridge overnight (remove the inner bowl from the slow cooker and pop in the fridge, covered with some cling film/plastic wrap).

The next day, scrape the set fat from the top of the soup and discard, or use for cooking. Remove the oxtail joints from the stew and remove the meat from the bones, discarding the bones, cartilage etc. as you go. Add the meat back into the soup.

Now you can either reheat the soup in the slow cooker, which will take a while, or transfer however much you want to eat to a saucepan or bowl and reheat on the hob or in the microwave. The slow cooker will have done its work by now, tenderizing the beef, so don't feel beholden to it, unless of course you want to!

Once warmed through, taste and adjust the seasoning if necessary, then serve with fresh bread.

Serves 8
–
Prep 45 mins
–
Cook 8 hours

SMOKY KOREAN BBQ BRISKET *

This is smoky, spicy and oh so good. Serve the brisket in slices, or shred it and mix it back in with the marinade for pulled Korean beef to stuff into burger buns. Don't use a rolled brisket for this – you want maximum exposure to the marinade, so flat is good.

150g (5½oz) tomato ketchup
50g (1¾oz) gochujang chilli paste
2 tbsp sesame oil
75ml (5 tbsp) rice vinegar
120ml (4fl oz/½ cup) dark soy sauce
2 tbsp maple syrup
1 tbsp ginger purée (paste)
1 tbsp garlic purée (paste)
12 spring onions (scallions), finely sliced, white and green parts kept separate
a few sprays of liquid smoke
vegetable oil, for frying
1.2kg (2lb 10oz) beef brisket joint
sea salt

To serve
cooked rice
a red chilli, sliced into rings
toasted sesame seeds

Preheat the slow cooker to LOW.

In a small bowl, combine the ketchup, gochujang, sesame oil, vinegar, soy sauce, maple syrup, and ginger and garlic purées and mix together until smooth. Tip them into the slow cooker and stir in and spring onion whites, a few spritzes of liquid smoke spray and a good pinch of salt.

Heat the vegetable oil in a large non-stick frying pan over high heat. Add the brisket and sear all over, turning it over with tongs, until browned and caramelized on all sides. Transfer it to the slow cooker and turn it over to coat in the marinade. Pop the lid on and cook for 7–8 hours, turning over halfway through cooking.

Serve with rice, drizzled with the marinade and sprinkled with the spring onion greens, toasted sesame seeds and chilli rings.

Tip
If you want a thicker sauce, tip the marinade into a saucepan and cook on the hob for a few minutes to reduce and thicken it before drizzling over.

Serves 6–8
–
Prep 20 mins
–
Cook 7–8 hours

BEEF WITH BEETROOT AND DILL ✳

Beetroot, beef and dill is one of my favourite combinations – they just work together somehow. And beef is rarely better than when it's slow cooked to tender perfection. Don't be alarmed by the addition of anchovies! They won't make the dish taste fishy, but instead impart a rich, savoury flavour. This is delicious served with mashed potatoes.

2 tbsp olive oil
700g (1lb 9oz) diced beef stewing steak
1 onion, finely sliced
1 large garlic clove, finely chopped
1 beef stock pot
a small can of anchovies in oil, chopped
600g (1lb 5oz) beetroot, peeled and halved, or quartered if very large
2 carrots, peeled and diced
2 celery sticks, sliced
a bunch of dill, roughly chopped
sea salt and freshly ground black pepper

Preheat the slow cooker to LOW.

Heat 1 tablespoon of the oil in a large non-stick frying pan over a very high heat and quickly brown half the beef until golden and caramelized on the outside. Transfer to the slow cooker with tongs and repeat to cook the remaining beef, adding the second tablespoon of oil. Transfer the second batch of beef to the slow cooker, leaving the fat in the pan.

Add the onion and garlic to the pan and cook for a few minutes until starting to pick up some colour, then add to the slow cooker.

Dissolve the stock pot in 200ml (7fl oz/scant 1 cup) of boiling water and use a little of it to deglaze the frying pan, tipping the liquid into the slow cooker along with the rest of the stock in the jug. Stir in the chopped anchovies, then add the beetroot, carrots and celery to the slow cooker, along with a good pinch of salt and pepper.

Cook 6–7 hours on LOW, or until the meat is really tender and the vegetables are cooked through. Stir in most of the dill, then taste and adjust the seasoning if necessary. Serve sprinkled with the remaining dill.

Serves 4
–
Prep 20 mins
–
Cook 6–7 hours

COFFEE
AND CHILLI
SHORT-RIBS *

These are a real crowd pleaser, and great for finishing off on a barbecue – or you can just put them under the grill (broiler). The meat, which just falls off the bones after its long cook, is given a delicious sweet glaze of chilli and coffee, which perfectly complements the beef. You'll need to think ahead for the long marinade and long cook, though.

12 short ribs (about 2kg/4lb 8oz)

For the rub
2 tbsp instant ground coffee powder
1 tbsp ancho chilli flakes
1 tbsp flaked sea salt
1 tbsp smoked sweet paprika
1 tsp garlic granules
1 tsp dried thyme
½ tsp freshly ground black pepper

For the glaze
4 tbsp soft brown sugar
1 tsp instant ground coffee powder
sea salt and freshly ground black
    pepper

In a small bowl, combine all the ingredients for the rub. Rub it all over the ribs, cover and leave to marinate in the fridge for up to a day.

Preheat a large 6-litre (6¼ quart) slow cooker to LOW.

Place the ribs into the cooker, snuggling them in so they all sit in one layer. Cook for 6–8 hours, until the meat is meltingly tender.

Once cooked, preheat the grill (broiler) to high and line a grill pan with foil. (Or you could also finish them off on the barbecue.)

Remove the ribs from the slow cooker with tongs and place them on the grill pan. Tip any juices from the slow cooker into a glass jug or bowl, leave to settle, then try and skim away as much fat from the top as you can. Tip the remaining juices into a saucepan and add the brown sugar and coffee powder. Cook for a few minutes until thick and syrupy. Taste and season with salt and pepper, if needed.

Brush the glaze over the ribs, then grill (or barbecue) for a few minutes until beginning to char and look glossy, before serving.

> Serves 6
> –
> Prep 30 mins,
> plus marinating
> –
> Cook 6–8 hours

Meat

LAMB SHANK TAGINE WITH BUTTERNUT AND POMEGRANATE *

If you want a really hearty portion, or for a meal to impress, serve a lamb shank each. But the four shanks will most likely stretch to six people. As you are spending on the shanks, it's well worth putting in a bit of extra time for prep here and browning everything beforehand. If you don't have a large slow cooker, just halve the recipe.

4 lamb shanks
3 tbsp ras el hanout
1–2 tbsp olive oil
2 red onions, sliced into wedges
2 tsp coriander seeds
3 large garlic cloves, finely chopped
2 cinnamon sticks
4 tbsp pomegranate molasses
1 tbsp butter
1 butternut squash, peeled and sliced into large chunks or crescents
a handful of mint leaves, roughly chopped
a handful of parsley leaves, roughly chopped
sea salt and freshly ground black pepper

To serve
buttered couscous with parsley and toasted almonds
pomegranate seeds

Preheat a large 6-litre (6¼ quart) slow cooker to LOW.

Pat the lamb shanks dry with kitchen roll (paper towel), if necessary, and sprinkle each one with ½ tablespoon of the ras el hanout. Heat 1 tablespoon of oil in a large non-stick frying pan and fry 2 of the shanks over high heat, turning regularly, until browned all over. Remove from the pan and transfer to a plate with tongs, then repeat to cook the remaining shanks, adding another tablespoon of oil if needed. Transfer to the plate, leaving any oil in the frying pan.

Add the onion wedges to the pan and sprinkle over the coriander seeds and remaining ras el hanout. Reduce the heat to medium and cook for a few minutes, turning halfway through, until they are picking up some colour. Tip them into the slow cooker.

Add the garlic and cinnamon sticks to the slow cooker, then pour in 300ml (10½fl oz/1¼ cups) boiling water. Add a good pinch of salt and gently mix. Place the lamb shanks into the slow cooker and drizzle half of the pomegranate molasses over them. Rub in roughly, then turn them over and drizzle the remaining molasses over the other sides, again rubbing in roughly. Push the shanks into the liquid so that they are half covered, then pop the lid on and cook for 5–6 hours on LOW.

Towards the end of the cooking time, melt the butter in the frying pan and add the butternut squash slices. Cook until lightly browned on the bottom, then turn over and cook until browned. Take the lid off the slow cooker and carefully remove the shanks with tongs. Give everything a good stir, then add the butternut slices to the cooker. Place the shanks back on top and cook for another 2 hours on LOW, until the butternut is cooked and the lamb is meltingly tender.

Taste and season with salt and pepper, then stir the herbs into the tagine, reserving a little to sprinkle over the top.

Serve the tagine with a pile of buttered couscous, sprinkled with the remaining herbs, toasted almonds and pomegranate seeds.

Serves 4–6
–
Prep 30 mins
–
Cook 7–8 hours

PERSIAN LAMB AND YELLOW SPLIT PEA STEW *

This aromatic stew, inspired by a Persian recipe called *gheymey*, is great for stretching out a little lamb, as the yellow split peas help to make it satisfying. Traditionally it would be served with chips or roasted potatoes and a pile of saffron rice.

2 tbsp olive oil
700g (1lb 9oz) diced lamb
1 large onion or 2 small, finely sliced
3 dried limes
160g (5¾oz) dried yellow split peas
5 tbsp tomato purée (paste)
sea salt

For the *advieh khoresh* (spice mix)
1½ tsp ground turmeric
1 tsp ground coriander
½ tsp ground cinnamon
½ tsp ground cumin
½ tsp ground cardamom
¼ tsp freshly ground black pepper
a good pinch of ground cloves
a good pinch of ground nutmeg

To serve
chips or roast potatoes
saffron rice
parsley leaves (optional)

Preheat the slow cooker.

Heat the oil in a non-stick frying pan over high heat and fry the lamb until browned, turning regularly – you may have to do this in batches, depending on the size of your pan. Transfer from the pan to the slow cooker with tongs, leaving the fat in the pan.

Meanwhile, combine all the spices for the spice mix in a small bowl.

Reduce the heat under the pan to low and add the onion to the pan. Cook for 5 minutes or so until beginning to soften, then add the spice mix and cook for a further few minutes until the onion is soft and picking up some colour. Tip everything into the slow cooker.

Pierce each of the dried limes a few times with a knife so the flavour can escape when cooking, then add them to the slow cooker along with the yellow split peas, tomato purée and 500ml (17fl oz/2 cups) boiling water from the kettle. Add a good pinch of salt and stir everything together well.

Cook for 3 hours on HIGH or 6 hours on LOW, until the split peas are well cooked and the lamb is really tender. Serve with roast potatoes or chips and saffron rice, sprinkled with parsley, if you like.

Tip
Dried limes are an essential ingredient for achieving the characteristic flavour of this stew. You can find them in the spices section of international supermarkets.

Serves 4–6
–
Prep 30 mins
–
Cook 3–6 hours

Meat

LAMB KLEFTIKO *

Lamb's soulmate seasonings – lemon, garlic and oregano – are all present in this classic Greek dish. For feeding a crowd, this is so easy; pop it on in the morning, ignore it all day and you'll have a delicious supper waiting for you. A simple Greek salad is the perfect accompaniment.

1kg (2lb 4oz) small potatoes
a good drizzle of olive oil
1 large lemon
1 tbsp dried oregano
2 tsp flaky sea salt
½ tsp freshly ground black pepper
2kg (4lb 8oz) leg of lamb
5 garlic cloves, halved or quartered
fresh oregano leaves, to serve

Preheat the slow cooker to LOW and tip the potatoes in. Drizzle over the olive oil and toss the potatoes to cover.

Finely grate the zest from the lemon. Combine it with the dried oregano and salt and black pepper.

Halve the zested lemon and squeeze the halves over the potatoes in the cooker, then chuck the squeezed shells into the cooker too.

Rub the lemon zest and oregano mixture all over the lamb. Cut small, deep slits all over the lamb leg and insert slices of the garlic. Place the lamb on top of the potatoes in the cooker and place the lid on. Cook for 8–9 hours, or until the lamb is meltingly tender.

Transfer everything to a serving platter and serve sprinkled with fresh oregano.

Serves 6
–
Prep 10 mins
–
Cook 8–9 hours

FRUITY GAME STEW WITH KALE AND DUMPLINGS ✲

A low-fat but rich gamey stew, topped with fluffy dumplings and a healthy share of veggies – this dish will make you feel nourished and leave you glowing with warmth in the depths of winter.

2 tbsp olive oil
800g (1lb 12oz) diced venison and other game
2 red onions, sliced
1 beef stock pot
2 tbsp redcurrant jelly
187ml (1 small bottle/6fl oz/¾ cup) fruity red wine
2 large carrots, peeled and chopped into chunks
2 large celery sticks, chopped into chunks
200g (7oz) chestnut (cremini) or mini portabello mushrooms, sliced
½ tsp juniper berries, crushed
1 rosemary sprig
1 bay leaf
2 tbsp cornflour (cornstarch)
100g (3½oz) dried cherries
200g (7oz) cavolo nero, sliced
sea salt and freshly ground black pepper

For the dumplings
180g (6¼oz/1⅓ cups) self-raising (self rising) flour
½ tsp baking powder
a good pinch of salt
80g (2¾oz/5½ tbsp) cold butter, cubed
80ml (2½fl oz/5½ tbsp) milk

Preheat the slow cooker to LOW.

Heat the oil in a frying pan over high heat and brown the diced venison and game, working in batches so you don't overcrowd the pan and everything caramelizes. Transfer to the slow cooker with tongs, leaving the oil in the pan.

Reduce the heat to low and add the onions to the frying pan. Cook for 6–7 minutes until picking up some colour, then transfer to the slow cooker.

Dissolve the stock pot in 600ml (21fl oz/2½ cups) of boiling water, then pour a little of the stock into the frying pan and use it to deglaze the pan, scraping the meaty juices from the bottom. Tip into the slow cooker, along with the rest of the stock from the jug.

Add the redcurrant jelly and red wine to the slow cooker and mix well until the jelly has broken down, then add the carrots, celery, mushrooms, juniper berries, rosemary and bay leaf and give everything a good stir. Add a good pinch of salt and pepper, then pop the lid on and cook for 6–7 hours.

Towards the end of the cooking time, prepare the dumplings. Put the flour, baking powder and salt into a large bowl and add the butter. Rub the butter into the flour with your fingertips until you have a mixture that resembles breadcrumbs. Add the milk and mix with a round-bladed knife until it comes together – you may need to use your hands towards the end to make sure everything is incorporated, but try not to overwork the mixture or your dumplings will be tough. Once it's a ball, knead gently for a few seconds until smooth, then divide it into 12 equal portions and roll each into a ball.

Ladle out a little of the juice from the slow cooker and put it in a saucepan over a low heat. Mix the cornflour with a little cold water, then add this to the saucepan. Cook for a few minutes until it starts to thicken, then stir it back into the stew.

Stir the dried cherries and sliced cavolo nero into the stew, then place the dumplings on top. Replace the lid and cook for another 1 hour until the stew is thickened and the dumplings are puffed up and cooked.

Serves 6
–
Prep 40 mins
–
Cook 7–8 hours

POULTRY

Like meat, poultry is rendered super tender when cooked in the slow cooker, and this chapter includes some classics, such as a cassoulet, teriyaki chicken thighs and even a "roast" chicken. But it's not just about whole joints or predictable soups and stews – slow cooked duck is perfect for the rillettes (pictured here), spread on crackers and served with pickles, or spicy buffalo chicken is pulled and piled into burgers with tangy blue cheese.

CREAMY TARRAGON CHICKEN WITH BACON, LEEKS AND POTATOES ✳

Creamy and comforting with a hit of aniseed sweetness from the tarragon, this is bound to become a firm family favourite.

2 tbsp olive oil
8 skinless, bone-in chicken thighs
6 rashers streaky bacon, chopped
1 large onion, sliced
2 large garlic cloves, finely chopped
3 large leeks, sliced
650g (1lb 7oz) small charlotte potatoes, unpeeled but halved if large
a small bunch of tarragon, roughly chopped, plus extra to serve
2 tsp wholegrain mustard
600ml (21fl oz/2½ cups) hot chicken stock
3 tbsp cornflour (cornstarch)
150g (5½oz) full fat crème fraîche
sea salt and freshly ground black pepper
cooked greens, to serve

Preheat the slow cooker.

Heat the oil in a non-stick frying pan over high heat and fry half the chicken thighs until browned all over. Transfer them to the slow cooker with tongs, leaving the oil in the pan and repeat to cook the remaining chicken, adding them to the slow cooker too. Add the chopped bacon to the pan and fry until crisp and golden. Turn the heat down to medium and add the onion. Cook for a few minutes until softened and picking up some colour, then add the garlic and cook for another 1–2 minutes. Tip the whole lot into the slow cooker.

Add the leeks, potatoes and half the tarragon to the slow cooker. Dissolve the mustard in the stock, then add it to the slow cooker. Mix the cornflour with a little cold water and stir that in too. Place the lid on the cooker and cook for 3–4 hours on HIGH or for 6–7 hours on LOW.

Once the casserole has had its cooking time, add the crème fraîche and the remaining tarragon and stir. Taste and adjust the seasoning, before serving with greens.

Serves 4
–
Prep 30 mins
–
Cook 3–7 hours

EASY CHICKEN PICCATA *

This classic dish with lemon and capers can be made so easily in the slow cooker. Simply brown the chicken in a pan, then chuck everything into the slow cooker and let it cook until tender and fragrant. You can use chicken breasts, rather than supremes, if you prefer.

2 tbsp butter
1 tbsp olive oil
4 chicken supremes
700g (1lb 9oz) baby potatoes, halved
    if large
finely grated zest of 1 lemon
    and juice of 2
2 garlic cloves, finely chopped
2 heaped tbsp drained capers
1 chicken stock pot
150ml (5fl oz/scant ⅔ cup) white wine
2 tbsp cornflour (cornstarch)
a small bunch of flat-leaf parsley,
    chopped
sea salt and freshly ground black
    pepper
green vegetables or salad, to serve

Preheat the slow cooker.

Melt 1 tablespoon of the butter in a large frying pan with the oil and add the chicken pieces. Cook over a medium–high heat for a few minutes, turning occasionally, until browned all over.

Tip the potatoes into the slow cooker and spread them out over the base, then transfer the chicken from the frying pan and place on top. Add the lemon juice and zest, garlic and capers.

Dissolve the chicken stock in 200ml (7fl oz/scant 1 cup) boiling water, then pour into the slow cooker followed by the wine. Add the remaining butter and a good pinch of salt and pepper. Cook for 6–7 hours on LOW or 3–4 hours on HIGH.

At the end of the cooking time, ladle out a little of the juice from the slow cooker and put it in a saucepan over a low heat. Mix the cornflour with a little cold water, then add this to the saucepan. Cook for a few minutes until it starts to thicken, then stir it into the juice in the slow cooker. Pop the lid back on and cook for another 20 minutes or so until it thickens. You can prepare some veggies to serve with it in the meantime.

Taste and check the seasoning, then stir in the parsley. Serve the piccata with green veggies or a salad.

Serves 4
–
Prep 20 mins
–
Cook 3–7 hours

Poultry

REVIVING CHICKEN NOODLE BROTH *

This is exactly what you want on a cold day if you're feeling a bit under the weather. You'll need a large 6-litre (6¼-quart) slow cooker for this. You can add some pak choi or shredded Chinese greens to the broth when you reheat it, if you like.

For the broth
1 large white onion, halved
stalks from a large bunch of coriander
1 large red chilli, halved
5 star anise
4cm (1½cm) piece of ginger, peeled and roughly sliced
2 garlic cloves, peeled but left whole and bashed
1 tsp black peppercorns
2 cinnamon sticks
1 whole small chicken
sea salt

To serve
200g (7oz) noodles (I like Udon)
toasted sesame oil, to drizzle
coriander (cilantro) leaves
sliced red chilli (optional)

Preheat the slow cooker to LOW.

First, add the aromatics to the slow cooker – the onion, coriander stalks, chilli, star anise, ginger, garlic, peppercorns and cinnamon sticks. Add a good pinch of salt and place the chicken, breast-side down, into the cooker.

Pour over 2 litres (2 quarts) of cold water and pop the lid on. Cook for 7 hours.

At the end of the cooking time, carefully remove the chicken from the broth with tongs, or whatever is easiest for you without burning yourself. It may break up as it's so tender, but that's fine as you're breaking it up anyway. Set aside until cool enough to handle.

Meanwhile, sieve the broth from the slow cooker into a clean saucepan, discarding all the veggies and herbs. If there is any chicken meat in the sieve, rescue it and pop it into the broth. Taste the broth and season – it will probably need a little more salt.

Once the chicken is cool enough to handle, strip the meat from the bones and add it to the broth. Reheat the broth and chicken gently on the hob, if necessary.

In a separate saucepan, cook the noodles according to the packet instructions, then drain and divide into bowls.

Ladle the broth over the noodles and finish with a drizzle of sesame oil, a few coriander leaves and some red chilli slices, if you like things hot.

Serves 6
–
Prep 20 mins
–
Cook 7 hours

TERIYAKI CHICKEN THIGHS *

As many of the poultry recipes in this book require a little prep, I was keen to have a real throw-it-all-in option. There's no chopping at all, and this dish can just be stirred up and thrown into the slow cooker in a few minutes in the morning before work and left to do its thing all day. The great sweet flavours do all the work. Serve with rice and simple blanched green veg or a salad.

100ml (3½fl oz/scant ½ cup) soy sauce
50g (1¾oz/¼ cup) brown sugar
2 tbsp honey
1 tbsp garlic purée (paste)
1 tbsp ginger purée (paste)
1 tbsp mirin
2 tbsp cornflour (cornstarch)
8 skinless chicken thighs
cooked rice and veggies or salad,
    to serve

Preheat the slow cooker.

In a bowl, stir together the soy sauce, sugar, honey, garlic and ginger pastes and mirin. Tip into the slow cooker.

Dissolve the cornflour in 50ml (1¾fl oz/3½ tbsp) water and tip that in too, then stir together well.

Add the chicken thighs to the slow cooker, turning them over so that they are coated in the sauce. Try and push as much of the meat under the sauce as possible.

Cook for 3–4 hours on HIGH or 7–8 hours on LOW, until the chicken is tender and the sauce is thickened.

Delicious served with rice and green veggies or a salad.

Serves 4
—
Prep 10 mins
—
Cook 3–8 hours

WHOLE "ROAST" CHICKEN WITH GRAVY AND CARROTS *

If you want to save energy and effort on your Sunday lunch, this is a good way to go about it. You can cook the chicken, gravy and carrots all at once, and you could even throw in some new potatoes at the beginning if you like, although I prefer to roast those separately. The chicken is so tender and moist – you don't have to worry about the breast drying out.

4 chunky carrots, peeled and cut into large chunks
1 large onion, cut into thick slices
1 lemon
1.5kg (3lb 5oz) whole chicken
a few thyme sprigs
a large rosemary sprig
2 bay leaves
20g (⅔oz) butter, sliced
2 tbsp cornflour (cornstarch)
sea salt and freshly ground black pepper
cooked vegetables, to serve

Preheat a large 6-litre (6¼ quart) slow cooker.

Put the carrots and onion slices into the base of the slow cooker to make a trivet for the chicken.

Halve the lemon and pop the halves into the chicken cavity, along with all the herbs.

Slide your fingers underneath the skin over the breast of the chicken to loosen it, then slide slices of the butter up and under it so that they are over the top of the breasts.

Place the chicken on top of the vegetables, then pour in 200ml (7fl oz/scant 1 cup) boiling water from the kettle. Mix the cornflour with a dash of cold water and stir until dissolved, then tip this into the slow cooker. Pop the lid on and cook for 3–4 hours on HIGH or 6–7 hours on LOW, until the juices run clear.

If you'd like to brown the chicken, preheat the grill (broiler) to high. Carefully (it will be very tender and almost falling apart at this point) remove the chicken from the slow cooker, tipping any liquid back into the cooker as you go, and place it on a baking tray. Place under the grill for a few minutes until browned. (Or if you have a slow cooker with a metal bowl, you can just put the whole bowl under the grill.)

Meanwhile pour the juice from the bowl through a sieve into a jug. Skim away any fat from the top with a spoon, then taste and season with salt and black pepper.

Serve the chicken with the carrots and gravy on the side, and other vegetables of your choice.

Serves 4
—
Prep 25 mins
—
Cook 3–7 hours

Poultry

49

PULLED BUFFALO CHICKEN AND BLUE CHEESE BURGERS *

Buffalo sauce teamed with blue cheese is an American classic, and the chicken is so easy to prepare in the slow cooker. Just chuck it all in and be ready for some smashing burgers once the time is up. It'll make four generously-stuffed burgers, or six normal-sized ones.

For the buffalo chicken
60g (2oz/4 tbsp) butter
100ml (3½fl oz/scant ½ cup) cayenne
  hot sauce, such as Frank's or Cholula
½ tsp garlic granules
1 tsp Worcestershire sauce
2 tbsp maple syrup
2 tbsp apple cider vinegar
a good pinch of salt
600g (1lb 5oz) skinless and boneless
  chicken thigh fillets

For the pink slaw
¼ small red cabbage, shredded
1 carrot, peeled and grated
½ small red onion, finely sliced
85g (3oz) mayonnaise, plus extra
  for the buns
sea salt and freshly ground black
  pepper

To serve
4–6 brioche burger buns
150g (5½oz) creamy blue cheese, sliced
a few lettuce leaves

Preheat the slow cooker.

To make the buffalo chicken, put the butter in the slow cooker to start melting while you gather all the other sauce ingredients. Add them to the slow cooker and stir together, then add the chicken and turn to coat in the sauce. Cook for 3–4 hours on HIGH or 6–7 hours on LOW until the chicken is falling apart tender.

While the chicken is cooking, make the slaw. Combine all the ingredients in a large bowl and season with salt and pepper.

Once the chicken is cooked, remove the thighs and shred the meat apart with forks. Return the shredded meat to the slow cooker bowl and stir well to coat in the sauce.

Toast the cut sides of your brioche buns in a dry frying pan or on a griddle, then spread the base of each one with a little mayo. Pile the chicken onto the base of each bun, top the chicken with a couple of slices of blue cheese and let it melt slightly into the hot chicken. Add lettuce leaves and finally the slaw. Replace the lid of the bun and serve.

Serves 4–6
–
Prep 20 mins
–
Cook 3–7 hours

CHICKEN MULLIGATAWNY

❄

A creamy, hearty Indian vegetable and rice soup which can be bulked up with whatever veggies you have to hand. The original recipe was thought to have a meat base, so I have included chicken thighs here for extra flavour and nutrients, and used a chicken stock base, but you could just as easily make this vegetarian by leaving the chicken out and using veggie stock – or vegan if you substitute the cream for a plant-based alternative.

1 large onion, finely diced
3 carrots, peeled and finely diced
2 celery sticks, peeled and finely diced
1 red (bell) pepper, deseeded and diced
1 eating apple, peeled, cored and diced
4 skinless chicken thighs
2 chicken stock pots
2 tbsp tomato purée (paste)
2 garlic cloves finely chopped
3cm (1¼in) piece of ginger, peeled and
    finely chopped
1 tsp ground coriander
1 tsp ground cumin
1 tsp ground turmeric
1 tbsp medium curry powder
90g (3¼oz) basmati rice
50ml (1¾fl oz/3½ tbsp) double (heavy)
    cream
sea salt and freshly ground black
    pepper
chopped parsley (optional), to serve

Preheat the slow cooker.

Add the onion, carrots, celery, pepper, apple and chicken thighs to the slow cooker. Pop in the stock pots and tomato purée, and add all the aromatics – the garlic, ginger, coriander, cumin, turmeric and curry powder. Pour in 1.4 litres (48fl oz/6 cups) water and pop the lid on. Cook for 2 hours on HIGH or 4 hours on LOW, or until the vegtables have softened and the chicken is cooked.

Add the rice and cook for a further 1 hour on HIGH or 2 hours on LOW, until the rice is cooked. Remove the chicken thighs from the cooker with tongs and shred the meat, discarding the bones and any inedible bits as you go. Return the chicken to the soup along with the cream and stir in, then taste and season with salt and pepper before serving sprinkled with parsley, if you wish.

Serves 6
—
Prep 30 mins
—
Cook 3–6 hours

Poultry

MEDITERRANEAN POT-ROAST POUSSIN ✳

This makes a great platter of food for a weekend roast or special occasion, but you don't have to use poussin – you could just as easily use chicken thighs. The lovely Mediterrenean flavours will all still be there.

2 tbsp olive oil
120g (4¼oz) smoked pancetta lardons
8 banana shallots, halved
1 garlic bulb, halved widthways
600g (1lb 5oz) charlotte potatoes, halved or quartered if large (no need to peel)
140g (5oz) marinated green and kalamata olives in oil
100g (3½oz) sundried tomatoes in oil
3 small rosemary sprigs
2 fresh bay leaves
2–3 poussin (depending on how large they are)
sea salt and freshly ground black pepper
green salad, to serve

Preheat the slow cooker to LOW.

Heat the oil in a large frying pan over medium–high heat and fry the pancetta for a few minutes until golden. Transfer the pancetta to the slow cooker using a slotted spoon, leaving the oil in the pan.

Next, add the shallots and garlic halves to the pan, cut-sides down, and fry for a few minutes until golden. Turn the shallots over and brown on the other sides, then add to the slow cooker. Add the potatoes, olives, sundried tomatoes, rosemary and bay leaves to the slow cooker, season, and give everything a good stir.

Finally, season the poussin well with salt and pepper, then fry in the reserved oil for a few minutes on each side until brown all over. Place the poussin on top of the vegetables in the slow cooker and pop the lid on. Cook for 5–6 hours on LOW until the vegetables are tender and everything is cooked through. Serve with a green salad.

Serves 4
–
Prep 25 mins
–
Cook 5–6 hours

SPICED DUCK, ORANGE AND HAZELNUT RILLETTES

This makes a fantastic autumnal starter at a dinner party to impress your guests. Or just keep them for yourself and pile them onto toasts, accompanied with pickles. If you seal the rillettes completely with the fat, they will keep in the fridge for a couple of weeks – and even get better for being matured a little. You can use a jar of duck fat, if you like, but I prefer to use good salted butter. You'll need six smallish ramekins (mine are 125ml/4fl oz/½ cup).

1kg (2lb 4oz) duck legs (about 3 meaty legs – I use Barbary/Muscovy ones)

For the salt rub
2 large oranges
2 tbsp flaked sea salt
1 tbsp dried thyme
1 tsp ground ginger
½ tsp freshly ground black pepper

For cooking and storing
3 sprigs fresh thyme
3 cloves, plus a few extra for the tops
2 cinnamon sticks
1 tsp coriander seeds, plus a few extra for the tops
1 tsp black peppercorns, plus a few extra for the tops
1 tsp allspice berries, lightly crushed, plus a few extra for the tops
3cm (1¼in) piece of ginger, sliced (no need to peel)
2 garlic cloves, bashed
200ml (7fl oz/scant 1 cup) good chicken or duck stock
50g (1¾oz) hazelnuts, toasted, plus a few extra for the tops
about 150g (5½oz) salted butter, melted, for covering

Serves 6
–
Prep 50 mins, plus marinating
–
Cook 6–7 hours

Preheat the oven to 100°C/200°F/gas mark ¼.

To make the rub, finely grate the zest from 1 orange and combine it with the salt, dried thyme, ground ginger and black pepper in a small bowl. Rub the mixture all over the duck legs, then cover them and place in the fridge overnight.

The next day, preheat the slow cooker to LOW.

Put the fresh thyme sprigs, cloves, cinnamon sticks, coriander seeds, peppercorns, allspice berries, ginger slices and garlic cloves in the slow cooker. Finely grate the zest from the remaining orange, then squeeze both oranges and add the zest and juice to the slow cooker, along with the stock.

Brush some of the salt rub off the duck legs (you want a bit to remain to season them, but removing some is good if you don't like things too salty) and add them to the slow cooker. Cook for 6–7 hours, until the duck legs are meltingly tender, then allow to cool until you can handle them comfortably.

Remove the duck legs from the slow cooker bowl and pour the juices in the cooker through a sieve into a jug. Discard the solids in the sieve and leave the gravy to settle, then skim the fat off the top with a spoon and discard. Shred the meat from the duck legs, discarding the bones and skin as you go, and put it in a bowl. Add enough of the duck stock to the bowl, so that you have lovely moist meat, but not so much that it's swimming in liquid (about 120–150ml/4–5½fl oz/8–10 tbsp should do it). Stir in the toasted hazelnuts, then divide the mixture between 6 small ramekins and press down firmly.

Pour the melted butter over the top of the ramekins, dividing it evenly between them so that it completely covers the meat. Use a little more butter if it doesn't quite cover them as the quantity will depend on your ramekins. Sprinkle a few of the spice seeds and the extra hazelnuts over the tops to decorate. Keep in the fridge, covered, until ready to serve, with pickles and toast or crackers.

DUCK WITH FIVE-SPICE, MARSALA AND PUY LENTILS ❋

Duck and Chinese five-spice are a great flavour combination in Asian-style dishes, but they also work with humble root veg and lentils in a brilliant winter warmer dish for cooler climes.

4 duck breasts
2½ tbsp Chinese five-spice powder
a drizzle of olive oil, if needed
2 red onions, sliced into wedges
220g (7¾oz) dried Puy lentils
500g (1lb 2oz) parsnips, peeled and diced
500g (1lb 2oz) carrots, peeled and diced
1 lamb or chicken stock pot
100ml (3½fl oz/scant ½ cup) Marsala or Madeira wine
sea salt and freshly ground black pepper
green beans or salad, to serve

Preheat the slow cooker.

With a sharp knife, cut several slashes through the fat on top of the duck breasts. Sprinkle about half of the five-spice over the duck breasts and rub in so that they are seasoned all over. Place the duck breasts, skin-side down, into a dry non-stick frying pan and set over a medium–high heat. As the pan heats up, it should start to render some of the fat from the duck. Once the skins have browned, turn the breasts over and cook for a few minutes on the other sides until browned all over. Remove from the pan with tongs.

If there's not much fat in the pan, add a drizzle of olive oil. Add the onions and cook for a few minutes until softened and picking up some colour, then transfer them to the slow cooker. Add the lentils, parsnips, carrots and the rest of the five-spice and stir everything together.

Dissolve the stock pot in 300ml (10½fl oz/1¼ cups) boiling water and pour into the slow cooker. Add the wine and season with salt and pepper, then place the duck breasts into the slow cooker, pop the lid on and cook for 5–7 hours on LOW, or 3–4 hours on HIGH, until the duck and lentils are really tender. Check the seasoning, then serve with green beans or salad.

Serves 4
–
Prep 25 mins
–
Cook 3–7 hours

DUCK CASSOULET *

Admittedly, this is a bit of a meat-fest, but it's so good – a French classic. You'll need a large 6-litre (6¼-quart) slow cooker to fit all the duck legs. If you are serving six people, add a couple of extra duck legs in, but the base will probably stretch to six as it's pretty generous. If you have any left, the bean and veggie mix is great piled onto toast the next day. The breadcrumb topping isn't actually traditional (or entirely necessary), but it does add a lovely crunch to the dish.

300g (10½oz) dried haricot or cannellini beans, soaked overnight
2 tbsp olive oil
250g (9oz) pancetta, in one thick slice, then diced into chunky dice
4 duck legs
6 French-style garlic sausages
1 onion, diced
4 large garlic cloves, sliced
2 chicken stock pots
1 × 400g (14oz) can chopped tomatoes
2 carrots, peeled and diced
2 celery sticks, peeled and diced
a few thyme sprigs
a couple of rosemary sprigs
3 cloves
1 thick slice of bread
1 tbsp butter
sea salt and freshly ground black pepper
green salad, to serve

The night before you want to make the cassoulet, pop the dried beans in a bowl and cover well with water. Leave to soak overnight.

The next day, preheat a large 6-litre (6¼-quart) slow cooker to LOW.

Heat the oil in a frying pan over high heat and fry the pancetta for several minutes until brown and crisp all over. Transfer to the slow cooker with a slotted spoon, leaving the fat in the pan.

Next, add the duck legs to the pan and fry until browned all over. Set them aside on a plate.

Add the sausages to the pan and fry until they are browned all over, then transfer them to the slow cooker.

Add the onion to the pan and fry for a few minutes until beginning to soften, then add the garlic and give it a couple more minutes before tipping into the slow cooker.

Dissolve the stock pots in 400ml (14fl oz/1¾ cups) hot water, then add to the slow cooker along with the tomatoes, carrots, celery, thyme, rosemary, cloves and a good pinch of salt and pepper. Give everything a good stir, then place the duck legs on top of the mixture. Pop the lid on and cook on LOW for 7–9 hours.

Towards the end of the cooking time, rip up the slice of bread, pop into a food processor and blitz to breadcrumbs. Heat the butter in a large frying pan until melted. Add the crumbs and stir so they are completely coated in the oil. Toast them over a medium heat for a few minutes until they are golden and crispy, then tip them out onto a plate.

Taste the cassoulet and check the seasoning, then serve topped with a sprinkling of buttery crumbs and a salad on the side to help balance it all out!

Serves 4–6
–
Prep 30 mins, plus soaking
–
Cook 7–9 hours

JERK TURKEY RICE

This is rice with a kick, but if you don't want it too hot, just add one Scotch bonnet and remove the seeds first. Even without in-your-face heat, there's still a delicious and aromatic ambient flavour from the allspice and thyme.

2 tbsp olive oil
1 red onion, finely diced
1½ tsp ground allspice
2 large cloves garlic, finely chopped
500g (1lb 2oz) turkey thigh mince
1 tbsp jerk seasoning
2 chicken stock pots
1 red (bell) pepper, deseeded and diced
1 green (bell) pepper, deseeded and diced
1 small can sweetcorn, drained
1–2 Scotch bonnet chillies, halved
1 × 400g (14oz) can red kidney beans, drained
leaves from a few bushy thyme sprigs, plus a few extra to serve
250g (9oz) American long grain rice
sea salt and freshly ground black pepper

Preheat the slow cooker to HIGH.

Heat the oil in a large frying pan over low–medium heat and add the onion and allspice. Fry gently for 5 minutes until the onion is softened. Add the garlic and cook for another minute or so, then add the turkey and jerk seasoning, turn the heat up to medium–high and cook until the turkey has browned. Tip everything into the slow cooker.

Add 200ml (7fl oz/scant 1 cup) water to the frying pan to deglaze it and dissolve the stock pots at the same time. Pour this into the slow cooker along with 550ml (19fl oz/scant 2½ cups) more cold water. Add the peppers, corn, Scotch bonnets, kidney beans, thyme and rice, plus a good pinch of salt and pepper.

Cook for 1½ hours until the rice is cooked through. Check it after 1¼ hours and reduce the cooking time if it feels like the rice is becoming at all mushy.

Taste and check the seasoning, then pile into bowls and serve sprinkled with extra thyme leaves.

Serves 4
—
Prep 30 mins
—
Cook 1½ hours

Poultry

FISH

A slow cooker probably isn't the most obvious way to cook fish, but you can get some brilliant results – from a no-fuss midweek dinner, such as tuna pasta or sweet and sour prawns, to something more impressive, such as a platter of salmon with charred spring onions and lime. You'll find plenty of inspiration here, as well as obligatory (and delicious) classics such as seafood chowder.

CREAMY TUNA AND PEA CONCHIGLIONI

This is such a simple midweek dinner. Try to use good-quality tuna steak which will hold together more than smaller flakes that will break apart completely. Both will be tasty, but I like to see discernible chunks of fish in there.

125g (4½oz) mascarpone cheese
400g (14oz) passata
2 tsp dried oregano
1 tsp dried basil
250g (9oz) conchiglioni pasta
   (large shells)
2 × 145g (5oz) cans tuna steak, drained
200g (7oz) frozen peas
sea salt and freshly ground black
   pepper
fresh basil leaves, to serve (optional)

Preheat the slow cooker to HIGH.

Put the mascarpone in a heatproof bowl and pour in 600ml (21fl oz/2½ cups) boiling water from the kettle. Stir until the cheese has melted into the liquid. Add the passata, oregano and basil and season well with salt and pepper.

Tip the pasta shells into the slow cooker and pour over the mascarpone and passata mixture. Stir everything together and try and make sure all the pasta is submerged under the liquid. Pop the lid on and cook for 1½ hours.

At the end of the cooking time, give everything a good stir, then taste and adjust the seasoning if needed. Add the tuna and peas to the slow cooker and stir in gently, being careful not to break up the tuna chunks too much. Replace the lid and cook for a further 30 minutes, then serve immediately sprinkled with fresh basil leaves, if you are feeling fancy.

Serves 4
–
Prep 15 mins
–
Cook 2 hours

Fish

COD WITH CHORIZO, POTATOES AND CHERRY TOMATOES

Chorizo is a great way to add flavour to simple white fish fillets. I've used cod here, but any similar fish – such as hake, coley or pollock – will work well. Throw in potatoes and some tomatoes and you have a complete meal in a pot. A mandoline is useful for the potatoes, or just some patience to slice them really thin. You'll also need a large 6-litre (6¼-quart) slow cooker, so that the potatoes are spread out and cook through properly, or halve the quantity for a small cooker.

2 tbsp olive oil
150g (5½oz) chorizo, sliced into discs
700g (1lb 9oz) new potatoes (I use Jersey royals)
3 small rosemary sprigs
4 cod fillets
4 cherry tomato vines (with 8 or 9 tomatoes on each)
sea salt and freshly ground black pepper

To serve
chopped parsley
lemon wedges

Preheat a large 6-litre (6¼-quart) slow cooker (preferably with a metal insert) to HIGH.

Heat the oil in a frying pan over medium heat and add the chorizo. Cook for a few minutes until it has released its oil and is starting to crisp up. Remove the pan from the heat.

Meanwhile, slice the potatoes into 2–3mm thick slices (no need to peel) using a sharp knife or ideally a mandoline. Put them in the slow cooker and add the chorizo and all the oil from the pan. Season well with salt and pepper and carefully mix it up so the potatoes are coated in the oil, then tuck the rosemary sprigs into the potatoes. Cook for 1 hour until the potatoes are starting to soften.

Place the cod fillets on top of the potatoes and season them, then finish by placing the tomato vines around them. Cook for a further 45 minutes–1 hour, until the potatoes are completely tender and the cod is cooked throughout. Serve with chopped parsley and lemon wedges.

Serves 4
–
Prep 30 mins
–
Cook 2 hours

COCONUT CURRY FISH PARCELS *

To prepare four of these parcels, you will probably need a 6-litre (6¼-quart) slow cooker so that they all sit flat and allow the carrots to cook through in time (I like to give them a quick blast in the microwave first, to start them off). Or you can halve the recipe and just make two parcels in a smaller cooker.

3 medium carrots, peeled and sliced
   very finely on the diagonal
8 large baby corn, halved lengthways
a large handful of mangetout (snow
   peas)
4 white fish fillets, such as cod, hake
   or coley

For the spice paste
2cm (¾in) piece of fresh ginger, peeled
   and roughly chopped
2 large garlic cloves, roughly chopped
3 lemongrass stalks
2 small Thai red chillies (or more if you
   want it hotter)
a bunch of coriander, stalks and leaves
juice and zest of 1 lime
2 spring onions (scallions), sliced,
   plus extra to serve (optional)
8 heaped tbsp coconut cream
salt

To serve
rice
lime wedges
sliced red chilli (optional)

Preheat a large 6-litre (6¼-quart) slow cooker to HIGH.

Blend the spice paste ingredients in a mini chopper or the small bowl of a food processor. If you can't fit the coconut cream in, you can just stir this in at the end once you have blended everything. Season well with salt.

Put the finely sliced carrots in a microwaveable bowl and add a splash of water. Microwave for 2 minutes on high, then add the corn and give it all another 2 minutes to start them off, or they can be a bit crunchy in the parcels.

Lay out 4 large sheets of baking paper. In the middle of each piece of paper, make a little trivet for the fish by spreading out a quarter of the softened carrots, then top with 4 halves of baby corn and a few mange tout. Place a piece of fish on top of each veggie pile, then spread a quarter of the spice paste over each one. Gather two sides of each sheet of paper and scrunch them together above the fish to create a sort of tent, trying not to disturb the paste on the fish, if you can. Roll in the sides to seal and place the parcels in the slow cooker, making sure each one sits flat on the base and they aren't piled up.

Cook for 45 minutes–1 hour, depending on how thick the fish fillets are, until the veggies are tender but still with a bit of a crunch, and the fish is cooked through. Serve with rice, lime wedges for squeezing over and extra chilli and spring onions, if you like.

Serves 4
–
Prep 30 mins
–
Cook 1 hour

CREAMY SEAFOOD CHOWDER *

Large pieces of fish and prawns in a creamy base make this classic soup indulgent and delicious. Use an all-rounder variety of potato (rather than a waxy type) and they will break down a little during cooking and help to thicken the soup.

1 tbsp olive oil
6 slices smoked streaky bacon, chopped
30g (1oz/2 tbsp) butter
1 onion, finely diced
1 fish stock pot
300g (10½oz) white potatoes, peeled and diced
2 bay leaves
2 tbsp cornflour (cornstarch)
100ml (3½fl oz/scant ½ cup) double (heavy) cream
160g (5¾oz) raw king prawns (jumbo shrimp)
360g (12¾oz) fish pie mix
a large handful of fresh parsley, chopped
sea salt and freshly ground black pepper
crusty bread, to serve

Preheat the slow cooker.

Heat the oil in a frying pan over a high heat and cook the bacon for 5 minutes until crisp and golden all over. Tip into the slow cooker.

Lower the heat and add the butter to the pan. Once melted, add the onion and sauté gently for about 8 minutes, or until really tender, then add to the slow cooker.

Dissolve the stock pot in 1 litre (35fl oz/4¼ cups) of boiling water, then add that to the slow cooker along with the potatoes and bay leaves. Mix the cornflour with a splash of cold water and stir until dissolved, then add to the slow cooker. Cook for 1½ hours on HIGH or 3 hours on LOW.

Add the cream, prawns and fish to the slow cooker and cook for a further 20 minutes on HIGH or 40 minutes on LOW.

Stir in the parsley, then season to taste and serve with bread on the side.

Serves 6
–
Prep 20 mins
–
Cook 2–4 hours

GALICIAN FISH STEW

Using fresh tomatoes here instead of canned gives this stew a lovely light flavour – perfect for serving on a summer's day with some fresh crusty bread and a glass of chilled white wine. If you can't find baby octopus, you can use octopus pieces – or substituting with squid will be delicious, too.

1kg (2lb 4oz) large fresh, ripe tomatoes
1 tbsp olive oil
1 onion, finely sliced
4 large garlic cloves, finely chopped
1 fish stock pot
1 red (bell) pepper, deseeded and
    sliced
400g (14oz) potatoes, peeled and diced
500g (1lb 2oz) octopus (baby octopus,
    whole or halved, or pieces)
250ml (9fl oz/1 cup) white wine
2 bay leaves
2 tbsp sweet smoked paprika
300g (10½oz) mussels in their shells
sea salt and freshly ground black
    pepper
fresh bread, to serve

Preheat the slow cooker.

Cut a cross in the base of the tomatoes with a sharp knife and pop them in a bowl. Pour boiling water over and leave for a few seconds, then fish them out with a slotted spoon and remove the skins – if the tomatoes are ripe, the skins should come off quite easily. Dice the tomato flesh, cutting out and discarding any tough, white core as you go, and tip them in the slow cooker.

Heat the oil in a non-stick frying pan over medium heat and add the onion. Cook for 6 minutes or so until softened, then add the garlic and cook for another couple of minutes before tipping into the slow cooker.

Dissolve the fish stock pot in 500ml (17fl oz/2 cups) boiling water, then add that to the slow cooker along with the red pepper, potatoes, octopus, white wine, bay leaves, smoked paprika and a good pinch of salt and pepper. Stir everything together, then pop the lid on and cook for 3 hours on HIGH, or 6 hours on LOW.

Meanwhile, clean and debeard the mussels, giving any that are open a short sharp tap as you go – if they don't close after a few seconds, discard them as they may be dead.

At the end of the cooking time, stir the mussels into the stew and cook for another 15 minutes on HIGH and 30 minutes on LOW, until they are cooked and have opened.

Taste and check the seasoning, then serve with crusty bread for dunking.

Serves 6
–
Prep 40 mins
–
Cook
3¼–6½ hours

SWEET AND SOUR KING PRAWNS

Sweet and sour prawns is one of my favourite takeaway dishes, but it always feels slightly artificial in flavour. Here is a lighter, slightly less sweet and far less alarmingly orange version, which is slow cooked but still has all the crunch and texture of your local takeaway's version.

50g (1¾oz/¼ cup) brown sugar
50ml (1¾fl oz/3½ tbsp) rice vinegar
125g (3½oz/½ cup) ketchup
1 tbsp soy sauce
1 tbsp oyster sauce
30g (1oz) cornflour (cornstarch)
100ml (3½fl oz/scant ½ cup) pineapple juice (from the can)
2 carrots, sliced on the diagonal
1 green (bell) pepper, deseeded and cut into large dice
1 red (bell) pepper, deseeded and cut into large dice
120g (4¼oz) baby corn, halved on the diagonal
8 spring onions (scallions), sliced into 2cm (¾in) lengths on the diagonal, white and green parts separated
100g (3½oz) drained canned pineapple chunks
100g (3½oz) mangetout (snow peas), whole if large or sliced in half on the diagonal
80g (2¾oz) canned sliced water chestnuts, drained
300g (10½oz) raw king prawns (jumbo shrimp)
sea salt

To serve
cooked rice
prawn crackers (optional)

Preheat the slow cooker to HIGH.

Stir together the brown sugar, vinegar, ketchup, soy sauce and oyster sauce in a small bowl or jug. Stir in the cornflour until smooth, then add the pineapple juice and 200ml (7fl oz/scant 1 cup) water.

Put the carrots, peppers, baby corn and spring onion whites in the slow cooker and stir in the sauce mixture. Replace the lid and cook for 1½ hours.

After this time, stir in the spring onion greens, pineapple chunks, mangetout, sliced water chestnuts and prawns and cook for a further 20 minutes, or until the prawns are just cooked. Taste and season, then serve with rice and prawn crackers, if you like.

Serves 4
–
Prep 30 mins
–
Cook 2 hours

SALMON WITH CHARRED SPRING ONIONS, GINGER AND LIME

The charred spring onions add a lovely smoky flavour to this easy salmon dish. It's simple but impressive enough to serve to guests as you can present the whole side on a platter. Serve with vegetables or salad, and perhaps some rice or bread.

12 spring onions (scallions)
1 tsp olive oil
2 limes
a side of salmon
½ fish stock pot
3cm (1¼oz) piece of fresh ginger, peeled and grated
30g (1oz/2 tbsp) salted butter
sea salt and freshly ground black pepper
coriander (cilantro) sprigs, to serve (optional)

Line a large slow cooker with baking parchment and preheat to HIGH.

Heat a griddle pan over a high heat. Toss the spring onions in the oil so they have a very light coating, then griddle them for a few minutes on each side until charred. Remove from the pan and set aside.

Slice one of the limes and lay the slices in the base of the slow cooker to act as a trivet for the salmon. Place the salmon on top, skin-side down. Dissolve the half stock pot in 100ml (3½fl oz/scant ½ cup) boiling water and pour it around the outside of the salmon.

Zest the remaining lime and put the zest in a small bowl with the grated ginger and butter. Beat them together then dot the flavoured butter over the salmon. Finally lay the charred spring onions on top and season well with salt and pepper.

Place the lid on the cooker and cook for 45 minutes to 1 hour, or until the salmon is just cooked and opaque throughout. Serve with the zested lime cut into wedges for squeezing over and sprigs of coriander to garnish, if you like.

Serves 4–6
–
Prep 20 mins
–
Cook 45 mins
– 1 hour

LITTLE SMOKED SALMON AND SPINACH EGG POTS

On a hungry day, I could happily eat two of these pots, so make as many as you feel. Serve with toast for a brilliant brunch or a quick (slow-cooker speaking!) supper.

160g (5¾oz) baby leaf spinach
80g (2¾oz) full fat crème fraîche
120g (4¼oz) smoked salmon, roughly chopped
4 free-range, organic eggs
chives, to sprinkle
sea salt and freshly ground black pepper
toast, to serve

Preheat the slow cooker to HIGH and find 4 small bowls or large ramekins – large tea or coffee cups will work, too.

Wilt the spinach for a few seconds in the microwave – about 20–30 seconds should do it – to take away some of its bulk so that you are more easily able to get it into the ramekins. Squeeze the wilted spinach between a few sheets of kitchen roll (paper towel) to remove any excess moisture, then divide it equally between the ramekins.

Put the crème fraîche into a bowl and season with a little salt (remember, the salmon is salty) and plenty of black pepper. Beat until smooth, then stir in the chopped salmon. Divide this evenly between the ramekins, spreading it out a little over the spinach, but keeping it away from the edges.

Finally, crack an egg into each ramekin, keeping the yolk intact and towards the centre of the ramekin – it will cook quicker if it touches the hot ceramic, so it may not stay runny, but if you prefer it more set, let it sit where it will!

Fill the slow cooker with enough boiling water from the kettle to come about halfway up the ramekins, then place the ramekins in. Replace the lid and cook for 20–30 minutes until the egg whites are cooked and set, but the yolks are still a little runny in the middle.

Sprinkle the pots with a few chives, and perhaps a little more black pepper to finish, and serve with toast.

Serves 2–4
–
Prep 20 mins
–
Cook 30 mins

Fish

GRAINS, PULSES & LEGUMES

Pulses and legumes are fantastic in the slow cooker as they are not too temperamental; dishes like the bonfire night baked beans, butterbean hummus and chickpea curry are tricky to overcook – they often seem to just get better as the flavours mature. Grains (and products based on grains, such as pasta) require a little more care so as not to become mushy, so just keep a closer eye on those, which is easier as their cooking times are much shorter.

CHEESY LEEK, THYME AND TALEGGIO RISOTTO

You have to be a little careful cooking risottos in the slow cooker as the rice does tend to become mushy quickly if you're not careful, but keep an eye on this and you will be rewarded with a creamy and delicious dinner.

30g (1oz/2 tbsp) butter
1 tbsp olive oil
1 large onion, finely diced
3 medium–large leeks, sliced (about 400g/14oz prepared weight)
3 large garlic cloves, finely chopped
leaves from a small bunch of thyme
280g (10oz) arborio risotto rice
150ml (5fl oz) white wine
800ml (28fl oz/3½ cups) hot chicken or vegetable stock (made with 2 stock pots)
150g (5½oz) taleggio cheese, rind trimmed off and ripped into pieces
50g (1¾oz) Parmesan cheese, grated, plus extra to serve
sea salt and freshly ground black pepper

Preheat the slow cooker.

Melt the butter with the oil in a large frying pan over medium heat. Add the onion and cook for 5 minutes until softened. Add the leeks, garlic and thyme and cook for another few minutes until softened, then tip everything into the slow cooker. Add the rice and stir around to coat in the garlicky butter, then add the wine and hot stock and season with salt and pepper. Cook on HIGH for 1 hour, until the rice is tender.

Stir the taleggio and Parmesan into the risotto until melted. Taste and adjust the seasoning if needed, before serving with extra Parmesan to sprinkle over the top.

Serves 6
–
Prep 30 mins
–
Cook 1 hour

PEPPERONI PIZZOTTO

A gloriously easy, throw-it-all-in dinner, this pasta-cum-risotto with pizza flavours is a real family favourite. Made largely with pantry staples, it can be made with little fuss on a weeknight.

280g (10oz) orzo pasta
500g (1lb 2oz) passata
2 tsp dried oregano
2 garlic cloves, minced
100g (3½oz) pepperoni slices
40g (1½oz) pitted black olives
100g (3½oz) jarred chargrilled (bell) pepper anti-pasti, sliced if pieces are large
120g (4¼oz) mozzarella cheese
sea salt and freshly ground black pepper
basil leaves, to serve

Preheat the slow cooker.

Tip the orzo into the slow cooker and add the passata, oregano and minced garlic. Top up with 400ml (14fl oz) of water and season really well with salt and pepper. Give everything a good stir then add the pepperoni, olives and red pepper and stir gently again to distribute evenly.

Cook on HIGH for 30 minutes. Give everything a good stir, then tear the mozzarella into small pieces and sprinkle over the top. Cook for another 30 minutes until the pasta is just tender (you can give it 10 more minutes or so if needed). Sprinkle basil leaves over the top and serve.

Serves 6
–
Prep 10 mins
–
Cook 1 hour

SPELT WITH BUTTERNUT, GOAT'S CHEESE AND WALNUTS ✲

This nourishing risotto-style dish brings together butternut and sage in a classic autumnal pairing. The cheese adds richness and another flavour pop, while the toasted walnut topping provides the crunch that is difficult to achieve in a slow cooker – and adding it later is perfectly acceptable!

2 tbsp olive oil
1 large red onion, finely diced
2 garlic cloves, finely chopped
1 vegetable or chicken stock pot
220g (7¾oz) pearled spelt
1 medium–large butternut squash, peeled, deseeded and diced into 2cm (1¾in) chunks
1 large eating apple, peeled, cored and finely diced
a small handful of sage leaves, shredded, plus a few extra to serve
a good pinch of chilli flakes (I use ancho, for a little extra smokiness)
75g (2½oz) walnuts, broken into pieces
120g (4½oz) crumbly goat's cheese
sea salt and freshly ground black pepper

Preheat the slow cooker to HIGH.

Heat the oil in a frying pan over medium heat and add the onion. Cook for about 6 minutes until starting to soften, then add the garlic and cook for 3–4 more minutes until everything is tender and beginning to pick up some colour. Tip it into the slow cooker.

Dissolve the stock pot in 700ml (24fl oz/3 cups) boiling water and add to the slow cooker, along with the spelt, butternut squash, apple, sage, chilli flakes and a good pinch of salt and pepper. Cook for 2 hours on HIGH.

Meanwhile, toast the walnuts in the oven or in a dry frying pan until smelling toasty.

After the 2 hours, the spelt should be tender but not mushy – still with a little bite – and the mixture still a little loose, like a risotto. Taste and check the seasoning, then divide it onto serving plates and crumble over the goat's cheese, letting it melt a little on the hot spelt. Sprinkle over the walnuts and finish with a little extra sage, to garnish.

Serves 6
–
Prep 30 mins
–
Cook 2 hours

CANNELLINI AND CHORIZO SOUP *

With creamy beans, smoky paprika and sweet peppers, this is one of my favourite soups – and is all the better for the fact that it can be made almost entirely from pantry staples. I love the satisfying chunks of chorizo and the flavour they add, but you can leave them out (and use vegetable stock) if you want to make it vegan.

250g (9oz) dried cannellini beans, soaked overnight (see method)
1 tbsp olive oil
150g (5½oz) chorizo, diced
1 large onion, diced
3 garlic cloves, finely chopped
1 large red (bell) pepper, deseeded and diced
400g (14oz) passata
1½ tsp dried thyme
¾ tsp dried rosemary
1 tsp smoked sweet paprika
2 chicken stock pots
sea salt and freshly ground black pepper
fresh thyme leaves, to serve (optional)

The night before you want to make the soup, pop the dried beans in a bowl and cover with water. Leave to soak overnight.

The next day, preheat the slow cooker.

Heat the oil in a frying pan over medium heat and add the chorizo. Cook for a few minutes until it has crisped up slightly and is staring to release its oil. Transfer to the slow cooker using a slotted spoon to keep the oil in the pan, then add the onion and garlic to the pan. Cook for 6–7 minutes until softened, then tip everything into the slow cooker.

Drain the beans and add to the slow cooker along with the red pepper, passata, thyme, rosemary, paprika and a good pinch of salt and pepper.

Dissolve the stock pots in 900ml (30½fl oz/3¾ cups) boiling water and add to the slow cooker, stirring everything together. Cook on HIGH for 4–5 hours or LOW for 7–8 hours until the beans are tender.

Taste and add more salt and pepper if needed, then serve scattered with fresh thyme leaves, if you like.

Serves 4–6
–
Prep 30 mins, plus soaking
–
Cook 4–8 hours

BONFIRE NIGHT MAPLE BACON 'BAKED' BEANS *

This makes a big batch, but it freezes really well and can be popped in the microwave to defrost and heat almost as quickly as taking a can of beans out of the pantry. Delicious piled into jacket potatoes and topped with cheese, or just serve on toast.

500g (1lb 2oz) dried haricot beans
12 slices smoked streaky bacon
2 tbsp olive oil
2 onions, finely diced
2 large garlic cloves, finely chopped
700g (1lb 9oz) passata
2 tsp smoked sweet paprika
4 tbsp maple syrup
sea salt and freshly ground black
    pepper

The night before you want to make the beans, pop the dried haricot beans in a bowl and cover with water. Leave to soak overnight.

The next day, preheat the slow cooker to LOW, and preheat the oven to 220°C/425°F/gas mark 7.

Lay the bacon slices on a baking tray (line it with foil to save on washing up, if you like). Place the tray in the oven and cook for 10 minutes or so, turning the slices halfway through, until the bacon is golden and crisp. Set aside until cool enough to handle, then chop it into small bits – this is easiest done with good kitchen scissors.

Heat the oil in a frying pan and add the onions. Cook for a good 8 minutes until tender and beginning to pick up some colour. Add the garlic to the pan and cook for another minute or so before tipping everything into the slow cooker. Drain the soaked beans and add to the cooker.

Pour the passata into the cooker, then quarter-fill the bottle with water and swill it about to pick up all the remaining tomato juice and tip that in too. Add the smoked paprika, maple syrup and a good pinch of salt and pepper and stir everything together.

Cook for 6–8 hours, or until the beans are tender. Check the seasoning and add more salt and pepper if needed, before serving.

Serves 6–8

–

Prep 30 mins,
plus soaking

–

Cook 6–8 hours

QUINOA, CORN AND PEPPER CHILLI *

For a nutritious and comforting supper, this chilli recipe is hard to beat. With quinoa for added protein, this veggie dish is substantial and satisfying. Serve with rice, pile into tacos or top a plate of nachos with the chilli, cheese and soured cream to make them 'loaded'.

2 tbsp olive oil
1 large red onion, finely sliced
2 large garlic cloves, finely chopped
2 red chillies, finely diced (include the seeds for more heat, or deseed), plus optional extra sliced chilli to serve
1 large sweet potato (about 250g/9oz), peeled and cut into 1.5cm (⅝in) dice
1 red (bell) pepper, deseeded and diced
1 green (bell) pepper, deseeded and diced
2 × 400g (14oz) cans chopped tomatoes
1 × 400g (14oz) can red kidney beans, drained
1 × 200g (7oz) can sweetcorn, drained
75g (2½oz) dried quinoa
1 veggie stock pot
2 star anise
1 tsp ground cumin
½ tsp ground cinnamon
1 tsp hot smoked paprika
sea salt and freshly ground black pepper

To serve
nachos, rice or tacos
grated cheese
coriander (cilantro) leaves
soured cream

Preheat the slow cooker.

Heat the oil in a non-stick frying pan and add the onion. Cook for about 6 minutes until softened. Add the garlic and chillies and cook for another minute or so, then tip into the slow cooker.

Add the sweet potato, peppers, tomatoes, kidney beans, sweetcorn and quinoa and stir everything together. Dissolve the stock pot in 300ml (10½fl oz/1¼ cups) boiling water from the kettle, then stir into the ingredients in the slow cooker along with the star anise, cumin, cinnamon and paprika. Season with salt and pepper and cook on LOW for 5–6 hours, or on HIGH for 3–4 hours, until the sweet potatoes are tender. Taste and adjust the seasoning if needed.

Serve the chilli – fishing out the star anise as you do – with nachos, tacos or rice, sprinkled with cheese and coriander and with a blob of soured cream on the side.

Serves 6–8
–
Prep 20 mins
–
Cook 3–6 hours

BUTTER BEAN HUMMUS WITH LEMON, GARLIC AND ROSEMARY

Dried beans come into their own when cooked in a slow cooker. Cooking them slowly in the seasonings means they reabsorb all the aromatics along with the water and it really adds a punch of flavour. Plus, buying beans dried is a more economical way to prepare them than ready-cooked in cans.

250g (9oz) dried butter beans
5 tbsp olive oil, plus extra for drizzling
finely grated zest and juice
    from 1 lemon
2 sprigs rosemary
2 garlic cloves, finely chopped
sea salt and freshly ground black
    pepper
bread, to serve

Put the butter beans in a bowl and cover with water and leave to soak overnight.

The next day, preheat the slow cooker to LOW.

Drain and rinse the beans, then peel off their skins. Tip the peeled beans into the slow cooker and add 250ml (9fl oz/1 cup) water and the olive oil. Add the lemon zest, rosemary and garlic and stir everything together. Pop the lid on and leave to cook for 4–6 hours, until the beans are broken down and soft (they should crush easily when pushed against the side of the slow cooker with a wooden spoon).

Once the beans are soft, pick out the rosemary stalks, then use a stick blender to blitz it to a purée – add a splash of water if it's too thick, and leave a few lumps if you like a bit of texture. Season really well with salt and pepper – beans will take quite a lot of salt – and add the lemon juice to taste.

Serve the beans swirled into tapas bowls, drizzled with a little extra olive oil, with fresh bread for dipping.

Serves 6

–

Prep 15 mins,
plus soaking

–

Cook 4–6 hours

WARM BELUGA LENTIL SALAD WITH SUNDRIED TOMATOES AND FETA

This is a satisfying 'self-dressing' salad. All the elements for the dressing cook along with the lentils so that they absorb all the flavours.

250g (9oz) beluga lentils
120g (4¼oz) jarred sundried tomatoes in olive oil, quartered or halved, depending on how big they are, plus 4 tbsp oil from the jar
3 tbsp good-quality balsamic vinegar
½ red onion, finely sliced
1 large garlic clove, finely chopped
1 tsp dried oregano
a large bunch of parsley, chopped
a large handful of mint leaves, chopped
70g (2½oz) rocket (arugula) leaves
160g (5¾oz) feta cheese
sea salt and freshly ground black pepper

Preheat the slow cooker to HIGH.

Put the lentils in the slow cooker along with the tomatoes and the 4 tablespoons of oil from the tomato jar, balsamic vinegar, onion, garlic and dried oregano. Pour in 300ml (10½fl oz/1¼ cups) water and stir everything together well, then pop the lid on. Cook for 1½–2 hours until the lentils are tender, but still with a little bite.

Fold the chopped herbs through the lentils and season generously with salt and pepper. Transfer the salad to a salad bowl and fold through the rocket leaves. Crumble the feta over the top of the salad and serve.

Serves 4–6

–

Prep 10 mins

–

Cook 1½–2 hours

TEA-INFUSED CHICKPEA *CHOLE*

✳

This is a version of a classic Punjabi dish which uses a spice that isn't that widely available outside of India, so instead you can use tea to mimic the flavour. It freezes really well, so this makes a large batch.

3 teabags (use a day-to-day blend, such as English breakfast)
500g (1lb 2oz) dried chickpeas
2 tsp cumin seeds
seeds from 6 cardamom pods
2 dried bay leaves
6 curry leaves
2 tsp ground coriander
2 tsp ground cumin
1 tsp ground cinnamon
½ tsp ground cloves
½ tsp ground turmeric
1 tsp chilli powder
3 tbsp olive oil
2 large onions, finely sliced
1 tbsp ginger purée (paste)
3 × 400g (14oz) cans chopped tomatoes
sea salt and freshly ground black pepper

To serve
cooked rice
fresh coriander (cilantro) leaves (optional)

Steep the tea bags in about 1 litre (35fl oz/4¼ cups) boiling water from the kettle. Leave the tea to brew for 5 minutes or so. Put the chickpeas in a bowl and pour the tea over (you can leave the bags in). Cover and leave the chickpeas to soak overnight.

The next day, preheat the slow cooker to LOW and drain the chickpeas.

Heat a frying pan over medium heat and add the cumin and cardamom seeds and the bay and curry leaves. Cook for a couple of minutes until beginning to smell aromatic. Add the ground spices and cook for another minute or so, then scrape everything into the slow cooker.

Add the oil to the pan and let it heat up over high heat, then add the onions and a good pinch of salt and cook for 10 minutes or so until they are softened and beginning to pick up some colour. Add the ginger paste and cook for another 30 seconds, then tip into the slow cooker.

Add the chopped tomatoes to the cooker along with 200ml (7fl oz/scant 1 cup) boiling water from the kettle. Stir everything together well, then pop the lid on and cook for 9–10 hours, or until the chickpeas are tender. The cooking time can vary hugely depending on the chickpeas, so just cook until they are tender – you can't really overcook this. Serve with rice and sprinkled with coriander, if you like.

Serves 6–8
—
Prep 30 mins, plus soaking
—
Cook 9–10 hours

VEGETABLES

Slow cooking is not just about tenderizing meat! There are tons of delicious vegetable-focused recipes you can try and the advantage is you don't have to wait so long as the cooking time is shorter – try the cauliflower korma or the vegetable pilau. But you can still slow cook in the true sense. The spiced red cabbage and French onion soup will both benefit from leaving their constituents to caramelize and infuse for a good amount of time, or try the shakshuka, which you can put in the slow cooker before you go to bed and wake up to a cooked breakfast.

WARMING ROOT VEG DAHL *

This is a great dish to have around – it can be a light lunch, a snack, or a more substantial dinner with rice and bread. It also freezes really well, so make a big batch (double the quantities if you have a large slow cooker) and freeze in individual portions for those times when you need something hearty and comforting and don't have the energy to cook.

2 vegetable stock pots
3 tbsp oil
1 large onion, finely diced
2 tsp ground cumin
2 tsp ground coriander
1 tsp ground turmeric
1 tsp black mustard seeds
1 tsp red chilli flakes, plus extra
    to serve
1 tbsp ginger purée (paste)
1 tbsp garlic purée (paste)
200g (7oz) carrots, peeled and diced
    (about 2 medium carrots)
200g (7oz) parsnips, peeled and diced
200g (7oz) sweet potatoes, peeled and
    diced
250g (9oz) dried red lentils
1 cinnamon stick
juice of ½ lemon
a large bunch of fresh coriander
    (cilantro), roughly chopped
sea salt
naan breads or rice, to serve (optional)

Preheat the slow cooker.

Dissolve the stock pots in 1 litre (35fl oz/4¼ cups) of boiling water in a jug and set aside.

Heat the oil in a frying pan over medium heat and add the onion. Stir to coat in the oil and begin cooking while you measure in the cumin, coriander, turmeric, mustard seeds and chilli flakes. Stir well and cook for a few minutes until the onion is browning and the spices smell aromatic. Add the garlic and ginger purées and cook for a couple more minutes before tipping the lot into the slow cooker.

Use a little of the stock to deglaze the pan, then tip that into the slow cooker along with the rest of the stock, root vegetables, lentils and cinnamon stick. Add a good pinch of salt and give everything a good stir. Pop the lid on and cook for 2–3 hours on HIGH or 4–5 hours on LOW until the vegetables are tender.

At the end of the cooking time, stir in the lemon juice, then add the coriander and more salt to taste – it will take quite a lot of salt. Serve on its own or with naan breads or rice.

Serves 4
–
Prep 30 mins
–
Cook 2–5 hours

SIMPLE SICILIAN CAPONATA

This is a classic Italian stew with the characteristic sweet and sour flavour from the vinegar. It is intended to be served at room temperature, not hot, like it's French cousin ratatouille. As the vegetables are quite bulky until they have cooked down, you'll need a large 6-litre (6¼-quart) slow cooker for this, or just halve the recipe.

2 celery sticks, sliced
2 large aubergines (eggplants), diced
4 large fresh tomatoes, diced
1 × 400g (14oz) can chopped tomatoes
1 red onion, sliced
2 red (bell) peppers, deseeded and
    diced
1 large courgette (zucchini), diced
3 tbsp red wine or sherry vinegar
1½ tbsp light brown soft sugar
2 tbsp drained capers
80g (2¾oz) green olives
4 tbsp olive oil, plus extra to serve
2 tbsp raisins
sea salt and freshly ground black
    pepper

To serve
basil leaves and bread

Preheat the slow cooker.

Put everything in the slow cooker and cook for 4 hours on HIGH or 6 hours on LOW.

Leave to cool to room temperature, then taste and season well with salt and pepper.

Top with basil leaves and perhaps an extra drizzle of oil, and serve as a salad with rustic bread.

Serves 4–6
–
Prep 20 mins
–
Cook 4–6 hours

Vegetables

CAULIFLOWER, CHICKPEA AND SPINACH KORMA

The mango chutney is optional here, but it adds a lovely hint of sweetness to this rich veggie curry. I use one with nigella seeds in, which adds a whole extra flavour dimension. You need to use really good coconut milk here with plenty of solids at the top, or the sauce will be too runny. If it is, stir in some ground almonds to thicken it up a little.

2 tbsp sunflower oil
1 large onion, finely diced
1 tbsp garlic purée (paste)
1 tbsp ginger purée (paste)
1 tsp ground cumin
1 tsp ground coriander
1 tsp ground turmeric
2 tbsp tomato purée (paste)
2 × 400g (14oz) cans good-quality, full fat coconut milk
1 large cauliflower, cut into florets
1 × 400g (14oz) can chickpeas, drained
1 cinnamon stick
4 cardamom pods, bashed
1 tbsp mango chutney (optional)
80g (2¾oz) bag of baby spinach
sea salt

To serve
basmati rice
chopped coriander (cilantro)

Preheat the slow cooker to HIGH.

Heat the oil in a frying pan over low–medium heat and sauté the onions for 6–7 minutes until softened. Add the garlic and ginger purées and the cumin, coriander and turmeric and cook for a couple more minutes until smelling toasty. Add the tomato purée and cook for a few seconds longer, then tip into the slow cooker.

Add 1 can of coconut milk to the slow cooker, along with the solids at the top of the second can (but not the liquid). Add a good pinch of salt and stir well. Add the cauliflower and chickpeas and stir again, then tuck the cinnamon stick and cardamom pods in the mixture. Pop a lid on and cook for 1½ hours, until the cauliflower is tender.

Stir the mango chutney into the curry, if using, then taste and add more salt if needed. Stir in the spinach, replace the lid and allow to wilt into the hot curry for 3–4 minutes, then serve with rice sprinkled with coriander.

Serves 4–6
–
Prep 30 mins
–
Cook 1½ hours

OVERNIGHT SHAKSHUKA *

Chuck all of this into the slow cooker before you go to bed and wake up to a delicious North African-style brekkie almost ready to go – you'll just need to add the eggs to cook for a few minutes while you pop the toast on.

2 × 400g (14oz) cans chopped tomatoes (or sub in one can cherry tomatoes if feeling fancy)
2 garlic cloves, finely chopped
1–2 tbsp harissa paste (depending how hot you want it)
1 tsp ground cumin
1 tsp ground coriander
1 tsp sweet smoked paprika
1 large red onion, finely sliced
1 red (bell) pepper, deseeded and diced
1 orange or yellow (bell) pepper, deseeded and diced
1 aubergine (eggplant), diced
4 eggs
sea salt and freshly ground black pepper

To serve
toast
a small handful of flat-leaf parsley

Don't worry about preheating the slow cooker for this one – it will have plenty of time overnight to heat up. Simply tip the tomatoes into the slow cooker and stir in the garlic, harissa, spices and a good pinch of salt and pepper to make a tasty sauce.

Pile all of the chopped vegetables into the slow cooker and stir so they are well coated in the tomato sauce. Pop the lid on the slow cooker, set it to LOW and leave for 8–10 hours overnight.

In the morning, taste the sauce and add more seasoning if needed. Make four wells in the mixture with the back of a spoon and crack an egg into each one. Replace the lid and cook for a further 15–20 minutes or so until the egg whites are cooked but the yolks are still runny.

Serve the shakshuka with toast and a sprinkle of parsley over the top.

Serves 4–6
–
Prep 15 mins
–
Cook 8½–10½ hours

Vegetables

CHILLI AND FETA CORNBREAD *

Using your slow cooker as an oven can save on power, so have a go at 'baking' in it. This tasty cornbread, with extra corn kernels, tangy feta and a chilli kick, is delicious served warm straight from the cooker or toasted the next day. Either way, make sure you slather it in plenty of salted butter.

125g (4½oz) plain (all-purpose) flour
2 tsp baking powder
1 tsp bicarbonate of soda (baking soda)
280g (10oz) cornmeal
1 tsp crushed chilli flakes
1 tsp fine sea salt
2 eggs
300ml (10½fl oz/1¼ cups) buttermilk
240ml (8fl oz/1 cup) milk
80g (2¾oz/5½ tbsp) butter, melted, plus extra for greasing and to serve
1 × 198g (7oz) can (165g/5¾oz drained weight) sweetcorn
100g (3½oz) feta, cut into small dice

Grease the metal bowl of a large 6-litre (6¼-quart) slow cooker with butter, then preheat it to HIGH.

Sift the flour, baking powder and bicarbonate of soda into a large mixing bowl and stir in the cornmeal, chilli flakes and salt.

In another bowl, whisk the eggs, then whisk in the buttermilk, milk and melted butter. Add to the dry ingredients and whisk together until smooth, then gently fold in the sweetcorn and feta.

Tip everything into the slow cooker and cook for about 1½ hours until risen and cooked through – check by inserting a skewer and making sure there is no raw batter on it.

Serve warm, slathered in more butter.

Serves 4–6
–
Prep 20 mins
–
Cook 1½ hours

AUTUMN VEGETABLE PILAU

This makes such a delicious and hearty dish. Have it as a side to meat, fish or a vegan option, or just enjoy a bowl of it as is, perhaps with a good dollop of thick yogurt.

½ tsp cumin seeds
1 tsp coriander seeds
3 dried bay leaves
4 whole cloves
2 cinnamon sticks
5 cardamom pods, bashed
½ tsp black mustard seeds
30g (1oz) butter
2 tbsp olive oil
1 large onion, finely sliced
1 leek, finely sliced
300g (10½oz) peeled and diced
    butternut squash (½ large squash)
2 large parsnips, peeled and diced
½ tsp ground turmeric
240g (8½oz) basmati rice
a good pinch of salt

Preheat the slow cooker to HIGH.

Toast the cumin and coriander seeds, bay leaves, cloves, cinnamon sticks, cardamom pods and black mustard seeds in a frying pan over medium heat for a couple of minutes until they are smelling toasty and fragrant, then remove them from the pan to a small bowl.

Add the butter and oil to the pan then add the onion and a good pinch of salt. Cook for a few minutes until beginning to soften, then add the leek. Cook for 5 minutes longer until the onion has really picked up some colour and the leek has softened.

Add the butternut and parsnips and cook for another few minutes, then add the toasted spices back in to the pan, along with the ground turmeric, and stir everything together. Tip everything into the slow cooker and cook for 1 hour.

Meanwhile, rinse the rice under cold running water and leave it to drain in the sieve. After the hour is up, add the rice to the slow cooker with 550ml (19fl oz/scant 2½ cups) water and cook for a further 1–1¼ hours, giving it a stir after 30 minutes, until the rice is cooked. Serve immediately, or remove from the slow cooker pot so it doesn't keep cooking and become mushy.

Serves 4–6
–
Prep 30 mins
–
Cook 2–2¼ hours

FRENCH ONION SOUP *

Caramelizing onions in a pan takes close vigilance to stop them burning. If you don't have a spare 40 minutes or so to stand at the stove, stirring, just stick them into a slow cooker and let it do the work for you.

40g (1½oz/2½ tbsp) butter
2 tbsp olive oil
5 large onions, finely sliced (about 1kg/2lb 4oz prepared weight)
1 large garlic clove, finely chopped
1 tbsp soft brown sugar
leaves from a few sprigs of thyme
2 rich beef stock pots or 1 litre (35fl oz/4¼ cups) really good beef stock
250ml (9fl oz/1 cup) white wine
1 tsp Worcestershire sauce
sea salt and freshly ground black pepper

For the cheese toasts
12 small slices of crusty white bread, such as baguette, sliced on the diagonal
salted butter, for spreading
200g (7oz) Gruyère cheese, grated

Preheat the slow cooker to LOW.

Melt the butter in the slow cooker and add the oil. Add the onions, then sprinkle over the chopped garlic, sugar, thyme leaves and a good pinch of salt and pepper. Stir everything together, then pop the lid on and cook for about 6 hours until darkened and caramelized. If you are around, give it a quick stir once in a while.

Once the onions are caramelized, make up the stock. If you are using rich beef stock pots, melt them in 1 litre (35fl oz/4¼ cups) of boiling water, or if you are using ready-prepared beef stock, simply heat it up. Add the stock to the slow cooker along with the white wine and Worcestershire sauce and cook for a further 30 minutes–1 hour until everything is well infused.

Towards the end of the cooking time, preheat the grill (broiler) and toast the bread on both sides until lightly golden all over, then spread with butter. If you have serving bowls that will be ok under the grill, fill them with soup and float 2 toasts on the top of each one. Pile on the cheese and melt it under the grill. Otherwise, you can just pile the cheese onto the toasts and melt it under the grill (I recommend putting them on a piece of foil so it doesn't make a mess of your grill pan!), and then pop the cheese toasts onto the top of bowls of soup to serve.

Serves 4–6
–
Prep 30 mins
–
Cook 7–7½ hours

Vegetables

MUSHROOM AND MASCARPONE MAC AND CHEESE

This is a very adult, creamy version of mac and cheese! At a push, you can put the mushrooms straight in the slow cooker, if you like, but I would definitely recommend a quick fry first to really bring out their flavour. You can buy packs of mixed mushrooms in more exciting varieties in the supermarket, but just use chestnut mushrooms, and slice them, if there are no interesting ones on offer.

250g (9oz) mascarpone cheese
70g (2½oz) Parmesan cheese, finely
    grated, plus optional extra to serve
1 tsp porcini powder
20g (⅔oz/1½ tbsp) butter
1 tbsp olive oil
400g (14oz) exotic mushroom mix
300g (10½oz) dried macaroni
120g (4¼oz) mozzarella cheese, grated
sea salt and freshly ground black
    pepper
green salad, to serve

Preheat the slow cooker to HIGH.

Put the mascarpone in a heatproof bowl and pour over 700ml (24fl oz/3 cups) of boiling water from the kettle. Stir until the mascarpone is melted, then stir in the Parmesan, porcini powder, a little salt and plenty of black pepper.

Melt half the butter with half the oil in a large frying pan over a high heat and quickly fry half the mushrooms until browned. Tip them into the slow cooker, then add the remaining butter, oil and mushrooms to the pan and repeat to cook the second half and tip them into the cooker too.

Add the macaroni to the cooker, then pour over the mascarpone mixture. Add the grated mozzarella and give everything a really good stir. Cook on HIGH for 1 hour.

After the hour is up, stir again and check how cooked the pasta is – you will probably need to give it another 10–15 minutes until it's really tender and any free liquid has been absorbed. Stir a final time and serve immediately with a green salad and an extra sprinkling of Parmesan, if wished.

Tip
Dried porcini powder is available at many supermarkets now, or online. It is pretty strong, but if you really like mushrooms, do increase the amount to your personal liking!

Serves 4–6
–
Prep 30 mins
–
Cook 1½ hours

CHRISTMAS-SPICED RED CABBAGE ✳

The original recipe for this was inspired by a Nigella Lawson dish I cooked years ago. It has evolved over the years and I've adapted it here for the slow cooker. It makes a classic Christmas side in our house, but you could serve it whenever really – it's also delicious piled into a jacket potato.

1 small red cabbage, shredded
2 onions, finely sliced
finely grated zest and juice of
    2 oranges
250ml (9fl oz/1 cup) red wine
4 tbsp soft brown sugar
1 tbsp flaked sea salt, plus extra
    to taste
2 cinnamon sticks
2 tsp ground mixed spice
100g (3½oz) dried cranberries
freshly ground black pepper

Put all the ingredients except for the cranberries in the slow cooker and give it a really good stir to combine.

Replace the lid and cook on LOW for 7 hours, or on HIGH for 3–4 hours, until the cabbage is tender. Add the cranberries, and cook for a final 30 minutes.

Taste and season with black pepper and extra salt, if needed.

Serves 8–10
–
Prep 20 mins
–
Cook 3–7 hours

SWEETS

Sweet recipes are, admittedly, not as simple to cook in your slow cooker as soups and stews, but I wanted to offer some real alternatives to simple poached fruit. So give them a go and be prepared to tweak the recipes for your own cooker. Raspberry cheesecake (pictured here) and frangipane peaches are perfect for a summer lunch in the garden, while a fruity ginger and chocolate sponge with custard or a comforting rice pudding are wonderfully warming on colder, darker days.

PEARS POACHED IN SAUTERNES AND VANILLA

Delicious warm with ice cream or crème fraîche, or enjoy cold later, these sweet pears, infused with vanilla and dessert wine, make a simple but sophisticated dessert.

100g (3½oz/½ cup) soft light brown sugar
200ml (7fl oz/scant 1 cup) Sauternes
pared zest of ½ orange
1 vanilla pod
4 pears, peeled, halved and cored
crème fraîche or ice cream, to serve

Preheat the slow cooker.

Put the sugar in a saucepan with 200ml (7fl oz/scant 1 cup) water and heat for a few minutes until the sugar dissolves and forms a very light syrup. Tip into the slow cooker and add the Sauternes and orange peel.

Split the vanilla pod lengthways with a sharp knife and scrape out the seeds; add them to the slow cooker along with the pod itself. Add the pear halves, spreading them out in as flat a layer as you can so they are all submerged in the liquid as much as possible.

Cook for 1½ hours on HIGH or 3 hours on LOW until the pears are tender, then remove them from the slow cooker. If you like, you can thicken up the poaching syrup a little and pour it over the pears to serve. Just pour it into a saucepan and cook over medium heat for a few minutes until thickened.

Spoon the pears into bowls and drizzle with the poaching syrup. Serve with crème fraîche or ice cream.

Serves 4
–
Prep 15 mins
–
Cook 1½–3 hours

Sweets

BANOFFEE RICE PUDDING ✳

The banoffee frills here are really just an interesting way to jolly up a reliable, staple recipe. You can, in fact, stir anything into this delicious creamy rice pudding to make it a bit more exciting – jam, berries, honey, etc – but this take is a firm favourite of mine. If you haven't got time to make the caramel sauce, don't sweat it – just buy it in.

For the rice pudding
butter, for greasing
150g (5½oz) pudding rice
1 litre (35fl oz/4¼ cups) whole milk
200ml (7fl oz/scant 1 cup) double (heavy) cream
50g (1¾oz/¼ cup) light soft brown sugar
2 tsp vanilla extract

For the caramel sauce
125g (4½oz) caster sugar
100ml (3½fl oz/scant ½ cup) double (heavy) cream
30g (1oz/2 tbsp) salted butter

To serve
2–3 bananas, sliced
grated dark chocolate (optional)

Grease the slow cooker with a little butter, then preheat the slow cooker to LOW.

Put the rice, milk, cream, sugar and vanilla extract in the slow cooker and stir everything together. Put the lid on and cook for 3½ hours, or until the rice is tender and the liquid is almost all absorbed, but the mixture is still loose and creamy.

While the rice is cooking, make the caramel sauce. Put the sugar into a saucepan and add 4 tablespoons water. Stir until the sugar has dissolved, then leave it to cook for 5 minutes or so, without stirring, until it is a nice caramel colour. Remove from the heat and add the cream and butter – it will bubble and spit at first, but keep stirring and it will come together into a smooth sauce.

Spoon the rice pudding into bowls and top with the sliced banana and a drizzle of warm caramel sauce. Finish with chocolate gratings, if you wish.

Serves 4
–
Prep 20 mins
–
Cook 3½ hours

STICKY GINGER AND CHOCOLATE SPONGE *

This sticky, dense sponge is brilliant if you want something home-baked about the house, as it's so versatile! Freshly steaming out of the slow-cooker (or reheated in the microwave – it freezes well) it is a great pudding with custard; have it as a satisfyingly rich fruit cake once it cools, or – if it's getting a bit old – slice, toast and enjoy served slathered with butter. I make this in a 3-litre (3-quart) slow cooker with a metal bowl insert.

2 ginger tea bags (I use Twinings Spiced Ginger)
350g (12oz) raisins
a little butter, for greasing
250g (9oz/heaped 1¾ cups) self-raising (self rising) flour
2 tbsp cocoa powder
½ tsp bicarbonate of soda (baking soda)
2 tsp ground ginger
a pinch of salt
175g (6oz) dark soft brown sugar
1 large egg, beaten
100g (3½oz) dark chocolate chunks
4 balls stem ginger, finely diced, plus 3 tbsp syrup from the jar

Make the tea using the 2 tea bags and 400ml (14fl oz/ 1¾ cups) hot water and leave to brew for a few minutes. Put the raisins in a large mixing bowl, then pour the tea over the raisins, cover the bowl with a plate and leave to soak for 2–3 hours.

Towards the end of the soaking time, grease a 3 litre (3 quart) slow cooker with a metal bowl with a little butter and preheat to HIGH.

Once the raisins have soaked and the cooker is hot, sift the flour, cocoa powder, bicarbonate of soda, ground ginger and salt into a bowl and set aside.

Stir the sugar into the raisin and tea mixture until dissolved, then beat in the egg. Stir in the chocolate chunks and diced stem ginger.

Tip the dry ingredients into the bowl with the fruit and fold everything together, then pour it into the slow cooker. Level the top with a spatula, pop the lid on and cook for 2½ hours, or until risen and a skewer inserted into the centre of the cake comes out clean. While still hot, prick holes all over the sponge with a skewer and drizzle the ginger syrup over the cake. Allow to cool a little and absorb the syrup, then remove from the slow cooker. Don't let it cool completely in there or it may stick.

Serve warm as a pudding with a little custard, or allow to cool and serve in slices, spread with butter if you fancy a little more indulgence.

Serves 10–12
–
Prep 30 mins
–
Cook 2½ hours, plus soaking

FRANGIPANE-STUFFED PEACHES

Slow-cooked sweet almond-scented peaches make a delicious dessert. If you want to add a bit more crunch, crumble some amaretti biscuits over the top before you serve.

4 large peaches
50g (1¾oz/3½ tbsp) butter, plus extra for greasing
50g (1¾oz/¼ cup) sugar
1 large egg
½ tsp almond extract
50g (1¾oz/½ cup) ground almonds
2 tbsp self-raising (self rising) flour
4–5 amaretti biscuits, crumbled (optional)
berries, to garnish
crème fraîche or ice cream, to serve

Grease a large 6-litre (6¼ quart) slow cooker with butter and preheat it to HIGH.

Halve the peaches and remove the stones, then place them into the slow cooker, cut-sides down. Cook for 45 minutes until softened and the cut sides are starting to brown a little, then turn them over.

At this point, start making the topping. In a mixing bowl, cream together the butter and sugar until light and creamy. Add the egg and almond extract and whisk until completely combined.

In a separate bowl, mix together the ground almonds and flour. Add this to the egg mixture and fold everything together.

Take the lid off the cooker and spoon a little frangipane into the hole in each peach, dividing it evenly between them. Place a tea towel (dish towel) over the top of the cooker to absorb the moisture, then pop the lid back on and cook for a further 30–45 minutes until the frangipane is risen. There will be some lovely crispy bits on the bottom of the cooker, so serve these into the bowls along with the peaches. Crumble a few amaretti biscuits over the tops of the peaches, if using, add a few berries and serve with a blob of crème fraîche or ball of ice cream.

Serves 4

–

Prep 20 mins

–

Cook 1½ hours

BOOZY CHOCOLATE HAZELNUT FONDUE

Fondues can be a little risky with all those open flames – whether it's around children or, as here, adults that may have already had a little too much. Using a slow cooker for the fondue is a great way of keeping everything warm whilst removing the chance of any accidents with the flames or gas burner. The heat is also more evenly spread out, so you stand a much lower chance of everything burning to the bottom.

400ml (14fl oz/1¾ cups) double (heavy) cream
100g (3½oz) blanched hazelnuts
200g (7oz) dark chocolate, broken into chunks
200g (7oz) milk chocolate, broken into chunks
150ml (5fl oz/scant ⅔ cup) Frangelico liqueur
strawberries, marshmallows, chunks of doughnut (or whatever else you want to dip), to serve

Put the cream in your slow cooker and turn it to LOW. Let the cream heat up with the cooker for 20–30 minutes.

Meanwhile, preheat the oven to 180°C/350°F/gas mark 4 and tip the hazelnuts onto a baking tray. Roast in the oven for 6–7 minutes, or until turning golden and smelling toasty. Allow to cool for a few minutes before roughly chopping.

Prepare whatever dunking goodies you have decided on and arrange on a platter.

Once the cooker is warm, add the chocolate and let it melt in the hot cream, stirring occasionally. Once it has melted, stir in the Frangelico.

Take the slow cooker to the table and sprinkle the chocolate mixture with the toasted hazelnuts. Allow people to dunk their own treats with fondue forks.

Tip
You could also use your slow cooker for a cheese fondue, too. The same benefits apply.

Serves 6–8
–
Prep 10 mins
–
Cook 40 mins

LEMON AND BLUEBERRY CLOUD PUDDING

This self-saucing pudding is the taste of childhood for me, so I'm so glad it works in a slow cooker. While it doesn't have the golden top I'm used to, it still has a fluffy lemon sponge on top of a delicious tangy custard. Slow cookers with metal bowls get a bit too hot for the custard, and can set it a little too fast, so ceramic bowls will work much better.

60g (2oz/4 tbsp) butter, plus extra for greasing
100g (3½oz/½ cup) caster sugar
2 eggs, separated
30g (1oz) cornflour (cornstarch)
280ml (10fl oz/generous 1 cup) whole milk
finely grated zest and juice of 1 lemon
75g (2½oz) blueberries

Grease a 3-litre (3-quart) slow cooker with a little butter and preheat to HIGH for at least half an hour (for this, the cooker needs to be really hot when the batter goes in).

Cream together the butter and sugar using a stand mixer or an electric hand whisk until really light and fluffy – this will take a good 5 minutes. Add the egg yolks and beat again until well combined.

Put the cornflour in a cup and add a splash of the milk. Mix to a smooth paste, then add it to the butter and sugar mixture, along with the remaining milk and the lemon juice. Mix again until everything is well combined. It will be quite a loose cake batter, but this is fine. It will also look a bit lumpy; don't worry – it will sort itself out whilst cooking!

In a separate grease-free bowl, whisk the egg whites until firm peaks are forming. Gently fold the egg whites into the cake batter, being careful not to knock too much air out of the mixture.

Scatter the blueberries into the slow cooker and pour the batter over the top. Place a tea towel (dish towel) over the top of the cooker to absorb the moisture, then pop the lid back on and cook for about 45 minutes–1 hour, until you have a fluffy sponge on top and a custard underneath. Serve immediately.

Serves 4
–
Prep 20 mins
–
Cook 45 mins – 1 hour

RASPBERRY, VANILLA AND DARK CHOCOLATE CHEESECAKE

Not only is raspberry, vanilla and chocolate a lovely combination of flavours, but the chocolate plays another roll – waterproofing the base until the topping starts to set so it doesn't become soggy. The flower decoration is optional, but it does make the cheesecake look worthy of an occasion.

For the base
200g (7oz) digestive biscuits (graham crackers)
80g (2¾oz/5½ tbsp) butter, melted
100g (3½oz) dark chocolate, melted

For the cheesecake
250g (9oz) mascarpone
400g (14oz) cream cheese
1½ tbsp vanilla bean paste
150g (5½oz/¾ cup) caster (superfine)sugar
3 eggs

For topping and decorating
400g (14oz) fresh raspberries
2 tbsp icing (confectioners') sugar
1 tbsp cornflour (cornstarch)
dark chocolate shavings
edible flowers (optional)

Preheat a large 6-litre (6¼-quart) slow cooker to HIGH. Place a clean tea towel (dish towel) in the bottom to use as a trivet, and pour in enough hot water from the kettle to come at least halfway up the sides of an 18-cm (7-inch) loose-based cake tin.

Once you have tested the water height, dry the tin and grease the inside, then line the base and sides with baking parchment. Line the outside of the tin with layers of cling film (plastic wrap) and foil, until you are sure you have made it watertight and no water will be able to seep into the cheesecake.

To make the base, put the digestives in a sturdy bag and bash with a rolling pin until you have fine crumbs. Tip them into a mixing bowl and stir in the butter and one-third of the melted chocolate. (You can also blitz the biscuits in a food processor and pour in the melted butter and chocolate to blend.) Tip the chocolatey crumbs into the prepared tin and press them down firmly – a potato masher is useful for this. Pour the remaining chocolate over the top and spread it thinly so it covers the surface of the biscuit, then pop the tin in the fridge for half an hour while you make the filling.

In a mixing bowl, gently whisk together the mascarpone, cream cheese, vanilla bean paste and sugar. Add the eggs and whisk again until you have a smooth mixture – be gentle as you don't want to whisk air into it – you are just combining the ingredients. Pour the filling over the chilled base and cover the top of the tin with a piece of foil. Transfer the tin to the slow cooker and cook for 1½ hours until set, but still a little wobbly in the centre, then turn the cooker off and let it cool in the cooker for another 1 hour. Then chill.

To make the topping, put 250g (9oz) of the raspberries in a saucepan and cook gently for a few minutes until they are beginning to break down. Tip the pulp into a sieve and push it through with a spoon to get rid of the seeds, then return the pulp to a clean pan and stir in the icing sugar. Mix the cornflour with a dash of cold water and stir it into the raspberry juice. Cook gently until it thickens to a sauce.

Pour the sauce over the cheesecake and spread out to the edges. Allow to cool, then decorate with the remaining raspberries, chocolate shavings and flowers, if using.

Serves 8
–
Prep 40 mins
–
Cook 2½ hours

INDIVIDUAL CRÈME BRÛLÉES

You will need four small (125ml/4fl oz) ramekins for this classic recipe, which needs just a few simple, good-quality ingredients.

275ml (9½fl oz/generous 1 cup) whole milk
1 whole egg, plus 3 yolks
40g (1½oz/scant ¼ cup) caster (superfine) sugar, plus extra to sprinkle and caramelize
2 tsp good-quality natural vanilla extract
shortbread and berries, to serve (optional)

Preheat the slow cooker to LOW. Find 4 small ramekins and fill the slow cooker with boiling water from the kettle, enough that when you come to place the ramekins in the cooker, the water goes three-quarters of the way up the sides – you want the water to be almost as high as the custard when they are filled.

Put the milk, whole egg and egg yolks in a jug and lightly beat them together. Add the sugar and vanilla bean paste and beat gently again until the sugar is dissolved. Let the mixture sit until the bubbles to disperse – you want the set custard to be smooth and not full of air.

Pour the custard into the ramekins, dividing it evenly between them, and carefully transfer them to the slow cooker. Place a tea towel (dish towel) over the top of the slow cooker and place the lid on to clamp it in place – this will absorb the condensation and stop it dripping from the lid back into the puddings. Cook for 45 minutes, or until the custard almost set – it will still have a little wobble, but will set as it cools down. Carefully remove the ramekins from the hot water and leave to cool to room temperature.

Sprinkle the tops of the custards with a good layer of sugar, then blast them with a chef's blow torch or under a very hot preheated grill (broiler) until the sugar browns and caramelizes. Serve straight away while the caramelized topping is still crisp, with shortbread alongside and berries to decorate, if wished.

Tip

You can make these in advance and just keep them in the fridge until ready to serve – although they are nicer if you let them come back to room temperature before serving. Sprinkle with sugar and brulée them just before you serve.

Serves 4
–
Prep 10 mins
–
Cook 45 mins

Sweets

SLOW COOKER *GLÖGG*

This Swedish mulled wine has a real kick from the spirit and is served with a few extras – raisins and almonds. Toasting the almonds isn't entirely authentic, but it adds an extra toasty flavour.

80ml (2¾oz/5½ tbsp) vodka or aquavit
100g (3½oz/½ cup) caster sugar
3 cinnamon sticks
pared peel of 1 large orange
10 cardamom pods, bashed
several slices of fresh ginger
6 cloves
a good handful of flaked almonds
1 × 75cl (26fl oz) bottle fruity red wine
raisins, to serve

Preheat the slow cooker to LOW. Add the vodka at this point to heat up with the cooker.

Once the cooker is warm, add the sugar to the slow cooker and stir. Once the sugar has dissolved in the liquid, add the spices. Pop the lid on and leave the boozy syrup to warm and infuse for a good 2–3 hours.

Meanwhile, toast the almonds for a few minutes in a hot oven or frying pan, until golden brown and smelly toasty.

Add the wine to the cooker and leave to warm up for half an hour or so, although it will sit happily on LOW (or the WARM setting if you cooker has one) for a couple of hours.

To serve, add a few raisins and a few toasted almonds to each cup, then ladle in the *glögg* and enjoy hot.

Serves 4–6
–
Prep 5 mins
–
Cook
2½–3½ hours

Sweets

INDEX

ACKNOWLEDGEMENTS

Tons of thanks to everyone involved in producing this book; to Stacey, Alicia and all at Quadrille, to Rita for the beautiful photographs, as ever, Max for the gorgeous props, and George, Sophie and Lara for their help in the kitchen. Thanks also to all my lovely friends and family taste testers, who can always be relied on for both kind words and honest opinions!